HUNTINGTON

A Search for its Roots

M. M. Stanley

Researched November 2002

First published in the United Kingdom in 2017
by C.C.Publishing (Chester)
Martins Lane, Hargrave, Chester, CH3 7RX
http://www.cc-publishing.co.uk

ISBN: 978-0-949001-59-7

3

Cheshire Coat of Arms

Map showing Huntington parish boundary

N

HUNTINGTON CP

Huntington

Saighton Camp

Eccleston

FOREWORD

For some years I felt Huntington should have a history of its own but it was overshadowed by Chester, probably inevitably. It was the black spot of the local history areas for some time. As I feel local history and family history are both of value and importance, eventually I just had to start investigating. It has been a considerable task but I hope those reading it will find it interesting and of some value.

Of course time moves on and changes occur. Since writing this, Huntington shops have changed hands. Gregson's post office and antiques business has gone and in its place is a very new home. The car sales garage is boarded up. It is many years since Reg Lowe's dance hall was on this site. There is no longer a butchers nor green grocers.

Great change has already taken place on the 'army' field at Saighton with houses appearing almost overnight. A new roundabout has been created to accommodate this. The forthcoming months and years will see further changes. Archaeological work, however, still goes on in Huntington which will add to the artefacts in the Grosvenor Museum.

Special thanks are due to all those who helped to make this publication possible. Thanks goes to Gordon Watkinson for unhesitating permission to use his plan of the Saighton village school. Throughout all my peregrinations in archives I had found no trace. I further wish to thank Mrs Julie Binnersley for her photographic contribution and also all those who kindly listened to my questions and gave of their knowledge, showing no boredom. I have so many names jotted down but sadly after such a time lapse, I cannot recall who said what. In spite of my lack of memory, however, I sincerely thank you all.

Finally, I offer thanks to my dedicated friend and IT advisor, Lynn, without whose interest and input preparing this work for publication would have been even more onerous.

Sincerely M. M. Stanley

CONTENTS

**CHESTER ROAD – HUNTINGTON LEADING
TOWARDS ALDFORD**

**CHESTER ROAD – HUNTINGTON LEADING
TOWARDS CHESTER**

ABSTRACT

At first sight Huntington village appears to have no particular significance or interest. It is two to three miles south-east of Chester and appears to be merely a through road, lined on both sides with straight rows of houses, that runs from Spital Boughton to the rural areas of Saighton, Bruera, Aldford, Farndon and beyond.

It is to be expected that it should be overshadowed by Chester with its historic wealth. The neighbouring settlement of Saighton also, although small, attracts interest from having been a seat of the Abbot of Chester, and in later years, from its connection with the Grosvenor family, but Huntington has not attracted similar study.

Huntington's position on the map, however, as one of a number of riverside settlements prompts a number of questions. Why has Huntington developed in the way that it has? It has considerably more population than all the surrounding areas yet St. Luke's church is of very recent date. Furthermore, with so much antiquity in the areas around surely there must be some history of its own to discover. Where does it fit in, or has it fitted in, in the scheme of things?

In studying the history of the area we need to look at the earlier church background with the ancient chapel of Bruera. Schooling, which centred on Bruera and Saighton, the pattern of landownership, plus the advent of the turnpike road, all enable pieces of this 'jigsaw' to gradually fit into place.

THE ANCIENT PARISHES, TOWNSHIPS AND
CHAPELRIES OF CHESHIRE

By F I Dunn, 1987 Produced by Cheshire Record Office

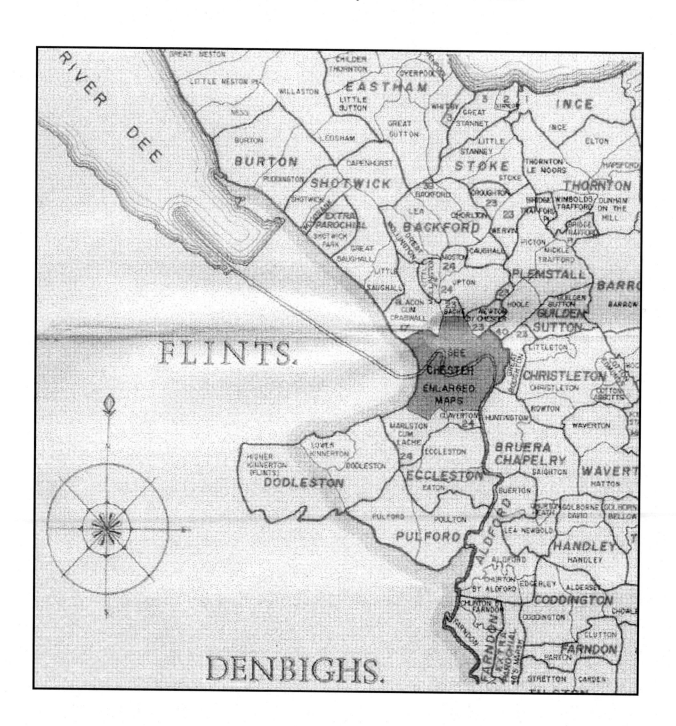

CHAPTER ONE

INTRODUCTION

The study of local history is worthwhile and educational. It
teaches about the past in terms of our locality and is thus
meaningful to each of us. It shows how our ancestors lived
and what problems they confronted, opens our eyes to the
infinitely varied pattern of the landscape and attempts to
explain how the present pattern emerged.[1]

Although the title of this study is "Huntington" and not "Huntington and Cheaveley",
because it is in Huntington that the dichotomy arose, it must be made clear that Cheaveley is a
hamlet in Huntington and as such is part of the study area. It is as Huntington cum Cheaveley
that it is referred in records. The connections with Saighton and Bruera also mean that all
these places will be referred to from time to time. They are all in the Hundred of Broxton.
Chester also, as the major town in Cheshire and because of Huntington's position on the edge
of the city, will inevitably be involved.

Due to Huntington and Cheaveley's "secondary" position in earlier relations with
Bruera and Saighton and especially as there is no Tithe Award available, this study has had to
rely heavily on Diocesan records for these areas, certain of the Grosvenor archives belonging
to the Westminster Estate and various local histories such as R.V.H. Burne's "Monks of
Chester". The Hincks family's private collection in the Cheshire Record Office provided
invaluable background for the Turnpike Trust and land-owning information.

Huntington cum Cheaveley was one of the manors in the possession of the
Benedictine abbey of St. Werburgh in Chester yet there is nothing in present day Huntington
that appears to be even an echo of the past. It is approximately three miles south-east of
Chester and gives the impression of being merely a through road, lined on both sides with

---

[1] D. Iredale, *Local History Research & Writing,* (Sussex, 1974), p.3

straight rows of 1930s houses, that runs from Spital Boughton on the outskirts of Chester to the rural areas of Saighton, Bruera, Aldford, Farndon and beyond. Furthermore, the township, or village as many locals call it, has inspired no local history publication and is considered a 'black spot', due to its lack of record, in the public library.

An analytical approach to the subject, bearing in mind Huntington's contiguity to the historic city of Chester and its Roman past, as well as to Rowton and its association with the conflict of the English Civil War battle there, led to a consideration of the township's situation as one of a number of settlements on the side of the River Dee. This progression of thought resulted in the conclusion that surely there must be some significance in the township's position, even though it may have been in earlier times than the period of this investigation.

Huntington cum Cheaveley was a component part of Saighton fee and attached to the Chapelry of Ease at Bruera. Saighton and Bruera both present a picture of the undeveloped and unspoilt village, although obviously changes have taken place there also. Huntington, on the other hand, although so close to them, and having had so much inter-connection with them, presents a very different appearance. As previously mentioned, its central development only began in the 1930s. Questions this investigation aims to answer are: Why at that time, and why so late? Why has this development happened in Huntington and not in Saighton and Bruera, although they are adjacent areas? Furthermore, why was this development restricted, until recent years, to this one section of Huntington?

It is to be expected, of course, that it should be overshadowed by Chester with its historic wealth and reputation. Yet why should it have been ignored in the published ranks of local histories? Surely it must hold some place in the history of the area?

As Huntington was once an Abbey possession, this study focused on the Dissolution of the Monasteries and then traced the changes in ownership from there. Without this record of descent, from Church ownership, to appropriation, and then down through the centuries of ownership, so much of understanding would have been lost. The investigation then progressed quite naturally into the ecclesiastical history of the area, with Bruera's, and thus

Huntington's, relationship with the Church in Chester and its authority. It led through the difficulties and differences that arose between the ancient chapelry and the church of St. Oswald in Chester and explained the causes and events of the intervening years between the early days of church attendance at Bruera and the noticeably late provision of the church of St. Luke, Huntington, in 1989.

A natural progression led to an attempt to trace schools in the area. The problem was that if a small school had existed there was every likelihood that no record would have survived. Once more the involvement of the Church provided guidance and some archival evidence. The involvement of the Grosvenor family added more. It was from such beginnings that the school at Saighton entered into the national education system.

Bad roads were a feature of many areas and probably none more so than at Huntington. The coming of the Turnpike Trusts must have brought many changes in their wake. A study of the Hincks collection at the Cheshire Record Office provided helpful information which gave an insight into the thoughts of a landowner at this period of time. The plans of the Chester - Farndon - Worthenbury Turnpike Trust have provided an excellent illustration of the route taken and of the owners and properties involved preparatory to, and during, construction. The specific direction of the route had been a source of local speculation and confusion for some time, posing the questions: Did it take the road to Saighton? Or was it the Aldford Road? The turnpike road development must have been a colossal endeavour without the benefit of modern machinery and without road-building experience. It was definitely another achievement by the 'sweat of the brow' and the back-breaking effort that was so much a part of life and labour before the introduction of labour-saving machinery and of so much that has been taken for granted in later years.

An analytical study of the nineteenth century, nationally as well as locally, led towards a realisation that it was not necessarily the demise of family lines, or of a desire for 'pastures new', that were the cause of such overwhelming changes in the pattern of land ownership. It aided a deeper understanding of the effects of the wide-ranging forces that pressed on all connected with agriculture in those changing and developing years.

The 1948 report on Huntington school has been included as it is an excellent description of the difficulties which were surmounted in that field and recalls the shortages of the war years which curtailed much of even small children's lives, not just their parents, and of the effects which lasted for some years afterwards. Furthermore, it epitomises much of the outside and 'outlying' nature and position of Huntington in and under the jurisdiction of distant authority. The inclusion of this particular account of education, at this particular time, not only adds to the atmosphere, and understanding, of the provision of schooling but also brings it smoothly into the present day.

This was a study that could not be hurried or skimped. Nor could it dwell totally on national influences and historical events and causes. Something of the 'personal' nature of peoples lives and their needs and desires had to be considered for history is not merely a list of dates or battles but an account, and an understanding, insofar as it is possible, of 'outrageous fortune' on every individual, whether great or small. In Hugh Trevor-Roper's words, it is 'the study not (only) of circumstances but of man in circumstances'.[2]

---

[2] L. Stone, *The Past & The Present,* (London, 1981) , p. 93

DOMESDAY CHESHIRE

L A N C A

(INTER RIPAM

Wallasey

• Great Meols
• Little Meols
• Upton
• Noctorum

Hilbre
Island

• Greasby
Grange
• Prenton
Landican
• Thingwall
Caldy
• Storeton
Thurstaston
• Poulton
Barnston
• Heswall
• Thornton Hough
Gayton • Raby
• Eastham
Leighton • Hargrave
Great Neston • Hooton • Overpool
• Hadlow III
• Little Neston
Ness • Ledsham • Sutton • Stanney
Burton • Capenhurst
• Puddington
• Croughton

Norton
Halton
Weston • Eanley
• Clifton
• Aston by Sutton
Frodsham • Middleton
Ince • Elton • Helsby • Kingsley
Thornton le Moors
Alvanley • 'Alderley'
Wimbalds Trafford • Dunham on the Hill
Wervin • Bridge Trafford • Manley

Gronant • Gwesbyr
Prestatyn • Golden Grove • Kelston
Rhydorddwy • 1. • Picton
Meliden • 2. Carnychan
Pentre • 3. Dincolyn • Axton
Cwyôr Bach • Bryn • Diserth • Trelawnyd
Cwybr • Whitford
Rhuddlan • Cefn Du • Hiraddug • Brynhedydd
Cyrchynan • Mertyn
Bodeugan • Bryngwyn
• Maenefa
St. Asaph • Biorant • Geilifyfdy Calcot
Cilowen • Tremeirchion • Trefraith • Brynford
Bodfari • Caerwys
IA • 'Radington'
Ysceifiog • Halkyn
• Trellyniau

Mostyn
Bychton
Greenfield
Bagillt • Coleshill
Leadbrook
Golftyn
Llys Edwin • Wepre
Soughton
Aston
IB
Hawarden
Broughton

Shotwick • Lea by Backford
Saughall • Great Mollington • Mickle Trafford
Little Mollington • Upton by Chester • Barrow
Blacon • Newton • Guilden Sutton
IV 'Redcliff' Great Boughton
CHESTER • Tarvin • Willington
Handbridge • Christleton
Overleigh • Netherleigh • Waverton • Clotton
Lache • Claverton • Huntington • Iddinshall • Tarporley
Marlston • Eccleston • Saighton • Foulk Stapleford
• Dodleston • Cheaveley • Hatton • Tiverton
Pulford • Eaton • Aldford • Golborne Bellow
• Leahall • Golborne David • Beeston
Poulton • Handley • Tattenhall • Spurstow
Allington • Chowley • Burwardsley • Peckforton
Radnor • Farndon • Coddington
Gresford • Hoseley • Clutton • Broxton
• Crewe Hall • Bickerton
Eyton • Duckington • Larkton
• Caldecott • Little Edge • Cholmondeley
Tilston • Edge • Bickley
Sutton • Shocklach
Overton • Hampton
Cuddington • Malpas • Norbury
Worthenbury • Tushingham • Marbury
• V • Wirswall
Erbistock

Ashton • Eddisbury

Eddisbury

II

Burwardestone • Whitchurch

Bettisfield

D E N B I G H S H I R E

R. Elwy
R. Clwyd
R. Alan
R. Dee

Hendrebifa
Bistre
Broncoed
• Rhos Ithel • Leeswood
Hope

1. Tan y Fron
2. Gwaunysgor
3. Llewerllyd
4. Trefedwen

Llystyn Hunedd
Mechlas
Llys y Coed
Gwysaney

HUNDREDS

IA	Atiscros (unhidated)	VII	Roelau
IB	Atiscros (hidated)	VIII	Riseton
II	Exestan	IX	Warmundestrou
III	Wilaveston	X	Tunendune
IV	Chester	XI	Middlewich
V	Dudestan	XII	Hamestan
VI	Bochelau		

Earl Hugh had demesne manors at places
underlined thus: _Eastham_

—— County boundaries of Cheshire, Flintshire (with
two detached parts) and adjoining counties 1880

S H R O P S H I R E

CHAPTER TWO

The Sixteenth Century

The earliest recorded reference to Huntington is in a charter of Edgar, King of the Mercians, dated 958, granting land at Huntington and Cheaveley to the collegiate church of St. Werburgh.[3]

Both Huntington and Cheaveley are recorded in the Domesday Survey as each of them having a small boat and a net which, although not specifically mentioning fisheries, is an implied reference to medieval fishing here.[4]

In the parcelling out of the manors contained within the present Hundred at the Conquest, the bishop was suffered to retain a moiety of Farndon, and the seculars of St. Werburgh, to keep Saighton, Cheveley, Huntin-don, Boughton, and moieties of Pulford and Wervin. Huntington was subsequently confirmed in 1093, with the other possessions of the seculars, to the Benedictine monks, who succeeded them in the abbey of St. Werburgh. The manor has been uniformly reputed since that period to be a component part of Saighton fee.[5]

Most of Cheshire before 1540 was either crown or monastic property so the redistribution of land is very much connected with the dissolution of the monasteries and the after-effects. This may pose the question: What has this to do with Huntington and its development? This study aims to show that it is in the history of the land and its ownership, together with other, and later, influences that the key to the puzzle lies. The Cheshire gentry (in this case) wanted wealth which meant land, as this, combined with education ensured social eminence, and after 1540 they gained much of it. Furthermore, to become a justice of the peace it was necessary to possess all three. Monastic lands in Cheshire had been well cultivated, for, from 1493 to 1538, John Birkenshaw, the abbot of St. Werburgh's, had improved the manor house at Saighton and imparked one thousand acres at Huntington,

---

[3] R.V.H.Burne, *The Monks of Chester*, (London, 1962), p.2

[4] Gen.Ed., J. Morris, Edited by P.Morgan, *Domesday Book, Cheshire 26*, (Phillimore, Chichester, 1978), p. 263 a, b

[5] G. Ormerod, *The history of the County Palatine and City of Chester, Ed. 2,revised T.Helsby* (London), p. 770

Cheveley (sic) and Saighton.[6] Clearly Huntington cum Cheaveley, as well as Saighton, was accounted desirable property.

Although charges about the extravagant lifestyle of abbots and monks were true, the situation has to be looked at in relation to the times and the requirements. Because of the size of the monastic buildings and the extent of their lands, they were essentially large estates with all the expense and administration that entailed. An abbot was chosen for his capabilities as an administrator of landed property and came from a social class that expected to hunt. In fact such abbots and monks expected a high standard of living. Furthermore, a large proportion of an abbey's expenses were in the payment of its bailiffs, many of whom, by the sixteenth century, came from the land-owning class, who gathered their rents in cash.

Other paid monastic officials were an auditor and 'honorary' stewards 'such as the Earl of Derby and the Earl of Shrewsbury who accepted annual pensions in return for protecting abbatial interests'.[7] Thus there were those of standing in the county who were well aware of land values and who, having worked for St. Werburgh's Abbey, were fully aware of its assets. It is thus evident that self-interest and profit play a part in this discussion of land and its influence on development in Huntington.

In 1534, the Act of Supremacy made the English Church independent of Rome. One of Henry VIII's first moves was made with regard to the religious communities, accomplishing the Dissolution of the Monasteries between 1536 and 1540. The real purpose of the Dissolution was financial, not religious. Henry VIII required money for his personal extravagance and also for the defence of the country. It was Thomas Cromwell's task to find it. The monasteries, with their wealth, and thus their unpopularity, presented an easy prey. In 1535, commissioners came to inquire into the income of the monastery. These were local men. One of Cromwell's chief visitors, Thomas Legh, who came afterwards and conducted the visitations, was descended from a Cheshire family. Amongst his unpleasant attributes he was also 'excessive in taking'.[8]

---

[6] J. Beck, *Tudor Cheshire,* (Chester, 1968), p. 96
[7] Ibid. p. 96
[8] R. V. H. Burne, *The Monks of Chester,* (London, 1962), p. 161

In June 1537 the abbot received a second request from Cromwell for the manor of Huntington to be granted to Master Edgeware, or failing that, the manors of Sutton and Ince. The abbot replied that "Nothing remains but the manor of Huntingdon, (sic) without which hospitality cannot be kept."[9] Once more this is evidence of Huntington as a desirable property and of its evident importance to the abbey. For the time being the manor remained in the abbot's hands. When it became clear that the monasteries were in jeopardy, however, St. Werburgh's monks tried to save what they could by leasing the manors they still held for large admission fines but low annual rental. Needless to say, there was no lack of takers.

It is interesting to note that on 18th October 1538 the manors of Huntington and Cheaveley were let to Thomas, Doctor Lee, (sic) by indenture for ninety-nine years.[10] Moreover, there was a postponement of the surrender of St. Werburgh's until more than a year had elapsed since the signing of his lease of the manors of Huntington and Cheaveley. Thus his lease was not affected by the Parliamentary Act which rendered all leases which had been made within a year of surrender null and void.

On 26th July 1541 the monastery of St. Werburgh was reconstituted as a Cathedral. Even so, all was not to be plain sailing. A rapid rise in wages and prices, due in part to the depreciation of the coinage by Henry VIII and his son, came to a completion when, in 1551, a Royal Proclamation announced the lowering of the currency. This diminution of income obviously affected the Cathedral so much so that it was reported by a Royal Commission that 'the Dean and Chapter had sold a great bell "which hanged in the new steeple there", the 4th of May, 1551 and also 'a cross and two silver censers on 31st January 1548 for £3 and used the money for the "reparacon of their houses".[11]

Then, in 1552-3, the Dean of Chester and two Prebendaries were imprisoned in the Fleet prison, by procurement of Sir Richard Cotton, Comptroller of the King's household. As Comptroller, Cotton had a seat in the Privy Council, the body investigating complaints about the sales of church property, which gave him his chance. After twenty days in prison the Dean, 'being dangerously syk of the gowte', was set at liberty, although his two companions

---

[9] R. V. H. Burne, *The Monks of Chester,* (London, 1962), p. 166
[10] Ibid., p. 171
[11] R. V. H. Burne, *Chester Cathedral,* (London ,1958), p. 23

were kept for another ten days. Shortly afterwards the Dean granted most of the Cathedral lands to Sir Richard Cotton for £603. 17s. 0d, although the rents of the property amounted to over £700.[12] It may have been the Commissioners' report that first suggested a chance for Sir Richard Cotton to enrich himself but he had seen his elder brother acquire Combermere Abbey at the Dissolution and no doubt he was on the lookout to collect for himself.

Among his many possessions were the manors of Huntington and Cheaveley, lands in Christleton, and the manor of Saighton with lands in Church en Heath, or Bruera. With cunning foresight he sold manors and lands to certain Cheshire gentlemen so that, when the new Dean and the Chapter tried to initiate proceedings, the case was complicated by having almost all the County against them. In the division of these, Saighton and Huntington became the property of George Beverley, of Huntington, later Sir George Beverley, knight.[13]

The monasteries in Cheshire, in this case notably St. Werburgh's Abbey, Chester, plus priories, churches, granges and other religious premises, had always assisted in the repair of roads and bridges because of their need to visit, travel and trade with each other and for administration purposes. There was a most severe setback at the time of Henry VIII's dissolution of the monasteries and all changed when the old monastic estates were broken up and divided into smaller compact units held by new owners who had no need to visit and travel all over the county. This resulted in a much reduced repair and maintenance of the roads and so their condition deteriorated rapidly.[14]

The roads were so bad, with many being impossible in winter, that the situation seriously impeded the improvement of the economy. Many of the population were so sympathetic to travellers and their problems that quite often those who could afford to, repaired some roads at their own expense, or left money in their wills for that purpose. In the early sixteenth century Sir William Stanley and Sir Hugh Calveley paid for the repair of 'two and a half miles of Huntington Lane from Boathill to Butterbache Bridge' as it was so bad and dangerous for pedestrians, wagons and those on horseback.

---

[12] R. V. H. Burne, *Chester Cathedral,* (London ,1958), p. 24
[13] Indenture
[14] K.W.L. Starkie, "The Evolution and Development of the Turnpike Road in Cheshire",
Cheshire History, p42

These names have passed out of use and possibly were lost with the turnpike development. Archdeacon Burne refers to "le untidynentindom de Saighton", which he says Morris translates as "Huntingdon Lane from Saighton".[15] If this is so then the present Sandy lane / Saighton Lane was once Huntington Lane and it would then seem that Boathill, named possibly from Eaton Boat, was the road that runs from Saighton, down to the Dee at Aldford.

In the section dealing with Buerton, which lies between Saighton and Aldford, Dodgson refers to *Bothill*, or 'hill near the boat',[16] which was named from the ferry at Eaton Boat. He adds that Huntington Lane was the main road from Chester to Aldford, maintained by the city and was referred to as *Chevely-Butter-back lane in Huntington.*[17] This might seem to favour the present Aldford Road having been the lost Huntington Lane but as the two roads are fairly close together it is possible that the old lane could have swung round to Saighton (which would have had some importance as a calling point) and then on down to Aldford and Cheaveley. Furthermore, there is evidence of a Roman road in that area.[18]

Later, in 1545, an act was passed authorising the two knights, or in their default, the Chester Corporation, to repair the highway as the need arose.[19] Examples such as these illustrate the perilous condition of the highways.

Until the middle of the sixteenth century the maintenance of roads was mainly a manorial responsibility but their appalling condition had been giving cause for anxiety and the result was that an Act, the Statute for Mending of Highways, came into force in 1555 and the manorial duty was passed to the parish, to be carried out by the parishioners under the supervision of unpaid Surveyors of Highways. Each parish was required to elect two honest people as Surveyors and every able-bodied lease-holder to either labour himself, or provide a substitute. Not surprisingly, many parishioners, particularly those in the smaller parishes, resented having to repair roads which were heavily used by complete strangers and there were many presentments of defaulters. What little result there was, meant that the roads, in most parts, worsened.

---

[15] R.V.H. Burne, *The Monks of Chester,* (London, 1962), p. 86

[16] J. McN.Dodgson, *The Place- names of Cheshire, Vol.XLVII,Part Four, (Cambridge,1977) p. 78*

[17] Ibid. p. 117

[18] Conversation with Keith Matthews, Chester Archaeologist.

[19] Cheshire History, No.39,1999-2000, p.29

CHAPTER THREE

The Seventeenth Century Turmoil and Change

The struggle between King and Parliament during the Civil War years of 1643-6 was a political issue and this dissension was a major turning point in the constitutional history of this country. It was a struggle for supreme power and the Parliamentary victory meant an end to the absolute powers of the monarchy, even after the Restoration. More was involved than the political issue though for it was inextricably linked with religious questions regarding the growing differences between Episcopacy and Presbyterians and Puritanism and Independence.

Chester, the largest town in Cheshire and protected by its walls and castle, was a Royalist stronghold throughout these years. It had the advantage of being on the flanks of Wales, also Royalist, and was a major road centre commanding the roads to the North Wales coast. Furthermore, the 'port' of Chester extended down the estuary and, most importantly, despite heavy silting in the upper portion of the Dee, these outposts were vital in bringing in food, supplies and reinforcements from Wales and Ireland, for the Parliamentarians had increased their hold on some of the main sea lanes. Nantwich, the second town of Cheshire and 23 miles away, was the headquarters of the Parliamentarian forces and was also a major road centre controlling routes from London to the north west of England and Wales. It, however, was very difficult to defend.

During the Civil War period the whole neighbourhood had been brought to a miserable pass and, as the war continued, the county became more impoverished. Huntington's close proximity to Chester, to Boughton, to Christleton where Sir William Brereton made his headquarters in December 1644, and to Rowton Moor, scene of the battle, must have meant a frightening involvement and untold suffering in the harsh and brutal passages of the war. There is confirmation of Huntington's involvement in a letter dated 30 April, 1645 that Sir William Brereton wrote of *our defensive works at ... Huntington,* among others.[20]

---

[20] R.H. Morris, *The Siege of Chester 1643-1646,* (Chester, 1924), p.100

THE CIVIL WARS IN CHESHIRE
R. N. Dore

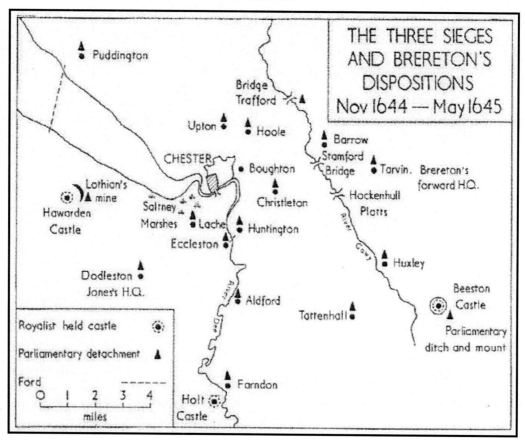

At a council of war held at Dodleston, 17th May 1645, to decide whether to continue the siege before Chester and Hawarden, or to withdraw, William Brereton left it to the discretion of two officers *whether Colonel Ashton's regiment march to ye body or march over ye boate at Eccleston and soe to Huntington ...* Before carrying out this resolution, Colonel Jones wrote to Brereton on several matters of importance and suggested that *because ye march will be too tedious for ye Lancashire foote I thinke it the best course for them to march to Huntington hall, thence to Tarvin.*[21]

The siege of Chester was long and the fighting bitter. Many houses in the eastern suburbs, along Eastgate and Watergate, were burnt by the occupants as part of a scorched earth policy. On 20th July 1643 a detachment from the Chester garrison made a sortie to Boughton (about a mile or so up the road from Huntington, leading into Chester) and turned the inhabitants (including the inmates of the hospital) out of their homes. The entire village was quickly razed to the ground by fire and demolition and with it the hospital, chapel and

---

[21] R.H. Morris, *The Siege of Chester 1643-1646,* (Chester, 1924), p. 88

several barns. This act of military necessity was accompanied by looting which resulted in bitter complaint from the displaced inhabitants and inmates to the Mayor. They protested that despite their known loyalty to the King they had not only been rendered homeless but were also robbed by their own soldiers - but all to no avail.

Then on 24th September the Royalist forces were soundly beaten at the battle of Rowton Moor, two miles to the south-east of Chester city and a 'hop, skip and a jump' from Huntington. Charles I himself watched the return of his broken and battered army. Indeed there are still people in Huntington who recall being told of the weapons and musket balls that were found up to fairly modern times in a field, near Saighton camp, which they called 'Death Valley'. It is said that a group of Royalist soldiers were overtaken by Roundheads here. Saighton camp, on the left, and Rowton, on the right, scene of the battle, can be clearly seen on the Ordnance Survey Street Atlas of Cheshire, 1995, between pages 59-60. It underlines the closeness of the battleground to Huntington.

Wars cost money, as well as lives. Parliament set out a quota of money to be contributed by each county. Cheshire was rated quite lightly, at just £175 per week under the first assessment ordinance of 1643. In many parliamentary counties assessments were by some way the main source of wartime income. In Cheshire, however, probably no more than £30,000 was raised via the national assessments during 1643-46/7. This was due to the fact that the county was quite small, far from wealthy, and until 1646 it was divided, with the richest part, its main town and its principal port, Chester, all in royalist hands.

Added to this direct taxation, Huntington and Cheaveley, in common with the Beverley family and all other people, towns, villages and townships, would have had to suffer the other costs of war, such as providing free accommodation, food and drink for the troops, together with seizure of war supplies, and plunder, the taking of horses, carts, crops, fodder, cash, household goods and so on. Feeding large numbers of soldiers was an ever-recurrent problem, as was also finding the money to pay them, and many men took it into their own hands to supplement such deficiencies.

Lennox Beverley, son of the founder of the Huntington Hall family, addressed a letter, dated 10th February 1643/4, to the Mayor of Chester, to say his sons had entered the King's service and that he had made heavy contributions in money and by provisioning troops quartered upon him, and thereby had to incur serious debts as *when all was at the best* he had but £24 a year for his family's maintenance. This letter provides a personal illustration of the disastrous and unhappy effects of the nation's differences on the people and is an indication of the straits to which the Beverley family, like many others, had been reduced by the Civil Wars.[22]

Hostilities finally ended after three years of civil war, yet in many ways the peace was sad and hollow. Crops had been trampled on, or commandeered, and cattle seized, year after year, for the soldiery; almost every horse had been taken for the cavalry. Supplies of every kind were in short supply and every one was war weary.

The Beverleys did not remain at Huntington. The estate was passed by purchase to Henry Harpur, Esquire; an attorney in the Exchequer of Chester. Nor were they the only ones to suffer as a result of the conflict. During the war and the period of the Commonwealth, a number of estates of royalist sympathizers were confiscated. Younger sons and even lesser squires found themselves unable to maintain their homes and families in their former state and abandoned the land for some more suitable profession, such as the law, or sank to the status of yeoman farmer. Many Cheshire gentry refused the knighthoods offered by the Commonwealth parliament and found themselves nearer to merging with a new, vigorous class of yeoman landowners. In the towns the Merchant and Craft Guilds offered opportunities to the ambitious. A new urban class was arising, with a new sense of power.

It is necessary in this modern day to understand something of the attitudes and expectations that were prevalent then regarding church attendance and conformity. The continuing strength of Catholicism was an issue of particular concern in seventeenth century Chester (and, indeed, elsewhere) and the government was in a constant state of anxiety about the situation in the counties of Cheshire and Lancashire. This concern is illustrated in an Order of the Quarter Sessions of 1682 that *divers persons of factious and discontented spirits and principles do upon sundaies and other holidaies, frequently if not constantly, absent*

---

[22] *Cheshire Sheaf,* 8 November 1939, p.99

themselves from the public worship of God used according to the Liturgy of the Church of England.[23]

The Toleration Act of 1689 opened the way for dissenting movements to gather force. Dissenters could meet legally in licensed meeting-houses from 1689 and Cheshire's widely-spaced parish churches provided the geographical conditions likely to encourage the provision of additional denomination churches in the wide churchless gaps.

The seventeenth century saw the initiation of coach services, thus underlining Chester's centrality in relation to land routes. The Cheshire Plain spans major routes from London to the north-west of England and North Wales. Chester was also mid-way along the western sea routes. The expansion of industry, trade and shipping at this time enhanced Chester's importance in the growing network of communications by land and sea. In 1637 the first coach known to run to timetable travelled between Birmingham and Holywell via Nantwich and Chester. Then in 1657 a service began between London and Chester which ran three times a week and took four days to complete.

The state of the roads continued to be appalling and caused Parliament to attempt to remedy the problem by restrictions on the use of narrow wheels which was considered to be a major cause of road damage. Thus an Act of 1662 ordered all cart wheels to be at least four inches wide. Then maximum loads, twenty hundred-weights in winter and thirty in summer, were fixed and no more than seven horses could be used to draw one load. This, however, was to no avail and it was left to the Turnpike Trusts to operate a rescue scheme for the county's poor roads which were vital to the developing trade, agriculture and industry of Cheshire.

A Turnpike Trust was essentially a body of people who were authorized by an Act of Parliament to repair a given length of highway, and were given powers to erect toll bars and to charge travellers and road users tolls to raise the necessary capital for the road works. The Trust could appoint surveyors, toll collectors, a clerk and a treasurer, and could also mortgage

---

[23] Cheshire Record Office, EDP 51/5

tolls in order to obtain funds more quickly.[24] Collection of tolls was one of the trustees' most troublesome duties because of the methods of collection and the complicated procedure governing the levying of tolls.

The first Turnpike Act came in 1664 on the Great North Road but the coming of the turnpike to Huntington had to wait another two hundred years, although Cheshire's first turnpike was early in the eighteenth century. This underlines the outlying, byway nature of Huntington's status and location.

---

[24] Starkie, K.W.L., "The Evolution and Development of the Turnpike Road in Cheshire", *Cheshire History,* p. 84

CHAPTER FOUR

The Eighteenth Century Developments

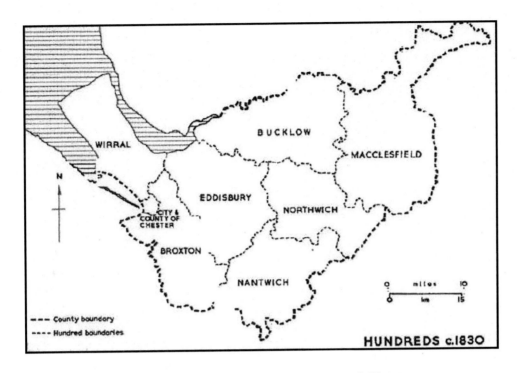

The Victoria History of the County of Chester

Cheshire remained overwhelmingly rural throughout the eighteenth century although the salt industry was expanding in mid-Cheshire and there were small textile industries growing up in the east of the county. It was still heavily dependent on its agriculture and in the Huntington area in particular. Cheese continued to be the main farm product and the market for dairy produce widened.

After the Jacobite rebellion in 1715 General George Wade was responsible for the smooth surfacing of 800 miles of road in Scotland, while in England the situation became increasingly urgent. The Government, with the safety of the realm in mind, and industry were on the march. Cheshire's first Turnpike Act in 1705 was only the fifth in England and Wales. It was but three and a half miles of the Chester to Whitchurch Road, now the A41, from Hatton Heath to Whitchurch Road. As late as 1775, however, Cole wrote that Cheshire roads were 'so worn and rugged that it is hardly safe much less easy to pass over them'…[25]

---

[25] Cheshire History, 1997-8, No. 37

The first half of the eighteenth century saw considerable investment in agricultural improvements and the variety undertaken bear witness to the concern of landowners with increasing the value of their holdings and farmers with raising the productivity of their lands, thereby to enhance their competitive position. The decline in agricultural prices during the 1730s and 1740s stimulated this investment as farmers and landowners sought to reduce their costs to meet the falling prices. During the 'depression' period landowners were often forced to assume financial responsibility for repairs and new construction of farm buildings, fences, gates, embankments and cottages, which were usually borne by their tenants in more prosperous times. Easier accessibility to wider markets, lower transport costs and the opportunity to shift the burden of road repair to the road users, recommended the turnpike to the small proprietor and the tenant farmer, as well as the larger landowner.

Chester's importance as a road centre continued throughout the eighteenth century but Huntington remained a byway. Most of the movement of trade and traffic to Chester from London and the Midlands entered the City along the roads which converged at Boughton Cross, a mile or so from the present centre of Huntington. In those days, however, and with the state of the farm tracks that were Huntington's 'roads', the advancement in roads and trade probably seemed far removed from the rural backwater. Huntington is not on a major route into Chester, hence its failure to grow.

Cheshire is a maritime county and all its waters converge on the two parallel estuaries of the Dee and Mersey rivers. Developing industry sought outlets to the Mersey for their commerce but the City of Chester lost its commercial importance to the rising port of Liverpool. Shifting sandbanks and the continued silting of the Dee, combined with opposition to improvements from local landowners, militated against any increase in Chester's trade. In fact the New Cut, made in 1732, between Chester and Wepre Gutter, canalizing the main channel near the Welsh coast to below Connah's Quay and thence to Parkgate, failed to save the port activities on Cheshire's side. Then in 1819, when the New Cut was extended to link the channel with the Mostyn Deep, it resulted in Connah's Quay taking most of the Dee traffic.

Apart from the estuaries of the Dee and Mersey and a few short stretches of river, Cheshire had no navigable inland waters. An Act was passed in 1722 for the construction of the Chester Canal from the Welsh Marches and the West Midlands with an outlet to the sea from the canal basin beyond the City's Northgate. Other canals followed of which only sections lay in Cheshire. The canals were a cheap, satisfactory means of transport for heavy, bulky, low-value goods such as building materials, coal, iron and manure as well as fragile, finished goods such as china and pottery.

The Ellesmere Canal was promoted in 1791 at the height of 'Canal Mania' by people with interests in the coal, iron and limestone of Flint and Denbigh who wanted access northwards to the Mersey and south to the Severn at Shrewsbury. It was opened in 1795 to passenger traffic and to goods in 1796. The junction with the Chester Canal was completed in January 1797. The building of the Manchester Ship Canal not only transformed the new township of Ellesmere Port, it meant that Chester dropped behind once more in commercial importance. It is realized, of course, that any development, or lack of development, in Chester is bound to have some effect on its surrounding areas, such as Huntington.

Although Bishop Gastrell, in his Notitia Cestriensis, provides the first definite information about the population of some parishes in the diocese in the early part of this century, recording numbers of families, Papists and Dissenters, sadly facts about Huntington are lacking. The only mention of it is as being part of the parish of St. Oswald, Chester.

Methodist societies were in Chester by 1765. By 1778, although Presbyterians, Independents and Quakers still maintained meeting-houses in Chester itself, except for the Independents, 'the most modern sect' whose meeting-house was 'new and neat', they were declining fast. Methodism, however, was spreading in the county. Indeed the Methodist expansion was the first indication of a dissenting revival which was to lead to dissenters rivaling churchmen in the county by 1851.

In its early years Methodism faced persecution. When a mob pulled down the Methodist preaching house in St. Martin's Ash, in the summer of 1752, the mayor refused to restrain or punish them. Sporadic persecution continued at Chester and other places but some societies benefited from the protection of landowners such as George Catton of Huntington Hall, who opened his house for preaching.

The late eighteenth and early nineteenth century was a time of unrest within the established Church of England. A time of change was well overdue for many people. Methodism gained many converts. The introduction of Methodism into the Chester area took place some years before Wesley himself visited the neighbourhood. He was preceded by one John Bennet, Assistant (Superintendent in modern times). Due to the rapidly-growing spread of Methodism with its resultant increase of work, it was decided in November 1749, at the Sixth Annual Conference, that one among the 'Helpers' appointed to a Circuit should have special responsibility and authority. An Assistant was responsible to Wesley and rendered accounts to him alone. This was the important position John Bennet held for the Cheshire Circuit which then also included Lancashire, Nottinghamshire, Derbyshire and parts of Yorkshire as far as Sheffield. Unhappily Bennet severed his connection with Wesley early in 1753 and there was widespread defection but the Methodists of Chester remained loyal to Wesley.

Infiltrations of Moravian doctrines into some of the societies and also John Bennet's break with Wesley in 1753 were more damaging to Methodism than persecution. Methodism, however, grew very rapidly in the county, despite these difficulties, partly because of its organization in circuits which enabled it to reach societies too small to support their own minister, or too isolated to share one with a neighbouring congregation. Although Huntington was not too isolated to be able to join with Bruera there seemed to be something in the Cheshire temperament that was attracted to Methodism.

Huntington cum Cheaveley, Saighton, Churton Heath (or Bruera) and Lea Newbold were all part of the Bruera chapelry, an ancient chapel of ease, in the Broxton Hundred and the deanery of Chester, belonging to the parish of St. Oswald, Chester, some miles away. Bruera, *capella de Bruwario,* 'the church on the heath', or latterly, Churton Heath. The modern form has been affected by that of Churton, three miles distant. The site of the chapel is in Saighton and a more ancient site may have been in Buerton.[26]

The ancient parish of St. Oswald covered a very large area. In 1831 it still stretched from Croughton, a hamlet four miles north of the city, to Lea Newbold, five miles to the

---

[26] Dodgson, *The Place-names of Cheshire,* pp. 115, 116.

south of it. On the west it included Crabwall three miles away and extended at least eight miles to the east to Iddenshall. It even included Hilbre Island, twenty miles away at the

ANCIENT PARISH OF ST OSWALDS

Published by The Institute and Genealogical Studies
Northgate
Canterbury, Kent, England

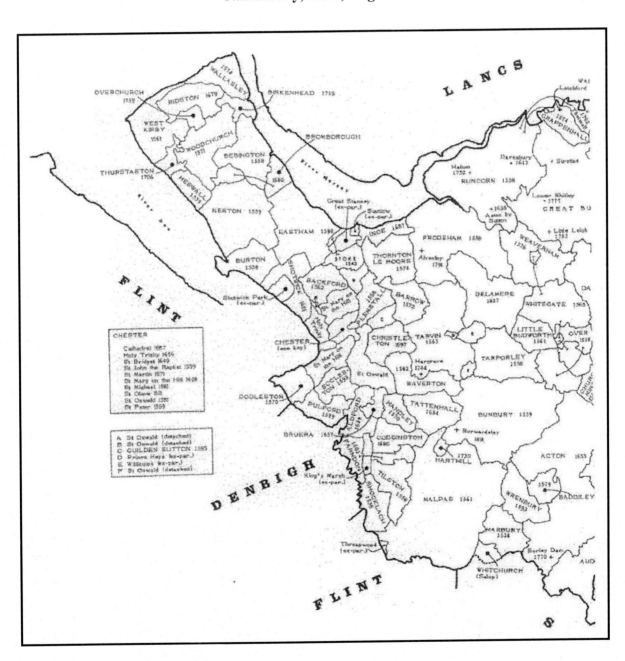

**CHURTON HEATH CHAPEL OR BRUERA
ON THE BOUNDARY**

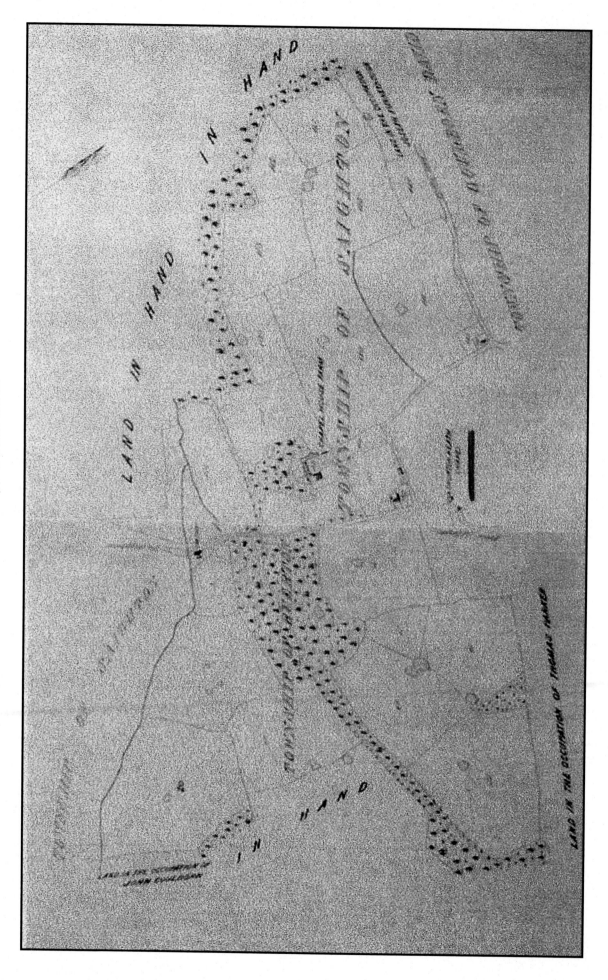

mouth of the Dee, off the Wirral coast.[27] The reason and connection is that they had all belonged to the abbey of St. Werburgh. Changes have occurred since then by having other parishes carved out of it and alterations to some parish boundaries.

The chapelry of Bruera (as it then was), stands about four miles south-east from Chester and approximately two miles from Huntington and was served by a stipendiary curate, appointed by the vicar of St. Oswald, who was presented to that vicarage with the chapel of Bruera annexed. It will be noticed that although the 'Mother Church' is called St. Werburgh, the vicar is of St. Oswald's. The congregation of St. Oswald's had no church of its own and in Saxon times had been housed in the church of St. Werburgh, belonging to the secular canons. When that church was replaced by the Benedictine abbey the parishioners still retained the right to use part of it for their church. St. Oswald was also an alternative title of the church, derived from the dedication of the altar within the abbey.

The questions asked in Bishops' Inquiries before Visitation reflect the concern felt by the established church authorities over the quality of religious life in the area. An examination of the Return written by the curate of Bruera, James Whinfield, in answer in 1778, reveals his statement that there were no papists or dissenters in the parish. The reply of 1789, which was made by the vicar, admits that there was one family of Papists but reports there were no dissenters or their meeting-houses.

By 1600 at least 23 grammar schools can be traced in Cheshire, with an unknown number of less formal and less ambitious establishments.[28] Much less is known about the local schools, the informal establishments which left - nor kept - few records. There is no precise knowledge of the earliest place or places of learning in the vicinity of Huntington. It is known, however, that there was a school in the village of Bruera in the eighteenth century, situated next to the church, because in February 1720 the Vicar, the Reverend Arthur Fogg, applied to the Bishop of Chester for a licence to enable his "Chappel clerk of Bruera", Robert Holland, "to teach school in the said Chappelry".[29]

---

[27] Burne, *The Monks of Chester*, p.23
[28] A. Crosby, *A History of Cheshire*, (Chichester, 1996), p. 78
[29] Cheshire Record Office, EDP 51 / 1 / 1

There is, however, no record of a specific foundation. The replies to the Inquiries before the Visitation of the Bishop add to the confusion which may owe somewhat to the situation of absentee vicars, then prevalent in the Church of England, and their ignorance of matters in their distant parishes. The pre-1789 Return[30] denies the existence of any school, whereas the 1789 Return[31] says that there is no free school but there is a small charity school.

BRUERA CHURCH

---

[30] Cheshire Record Office, MF 44 / 1
[31] Ibid, MF 44 / 5 / 2

CHAPTER FIVE

The Nineteenth Century Advancements

Roads and Transport

The Act of 1800 which brought Ireland into the United Kingdom increased the need for fast communication lines with Ireland, especially between London and Holyhead. The first parliamentary committee to deal with major through routes was appointed in 1810 and the Holyhead road was the first to be considered. Then in 1826 when road surfaces improved beyond recognition, thanks to Macadam's new methods of construction and surfacing, road-making spread throughout the country. This was the heyday of the coaching age which was to be short-lived for the railway era was at hand - but not at Huntington. Coaching was over by 1850 and the roads used only for local traffic. Yet it was at this late time that the turnpike through Huntington came under consideration. It is possible that this was due to Grosvenor interest as the Eaton Estate is 'just down the road' from Huntington.

A letter dated September 1850[32] was sent from the Road Office, London, to the Clerk to the Trustees, to call his attention to "An Act to continue certain Turnpike Acts in Great Britain, ... by which a Sinking Fund of five per cent per annum on the principal debt is required to be set apart by each Turnpike Trust ... and requesting him to bring the matter to the attention of the Trustees." This was to ensure a 'gradual extinction of the existing debt upon the Trust, without placing any additional burthens upon the Public Traveller, or upon the Landowners, and Rate-payers'. Furthermore, the Turnpike Trusts had to make Returns to the Secretary of State for the Home Department which, judging by a letter dated 1st October 1844, seem to have come under keen scrutiny.[33]

---

[32] Cheshire Record Office, TRT/8
[33] Ibid, TRT/7/4n

33

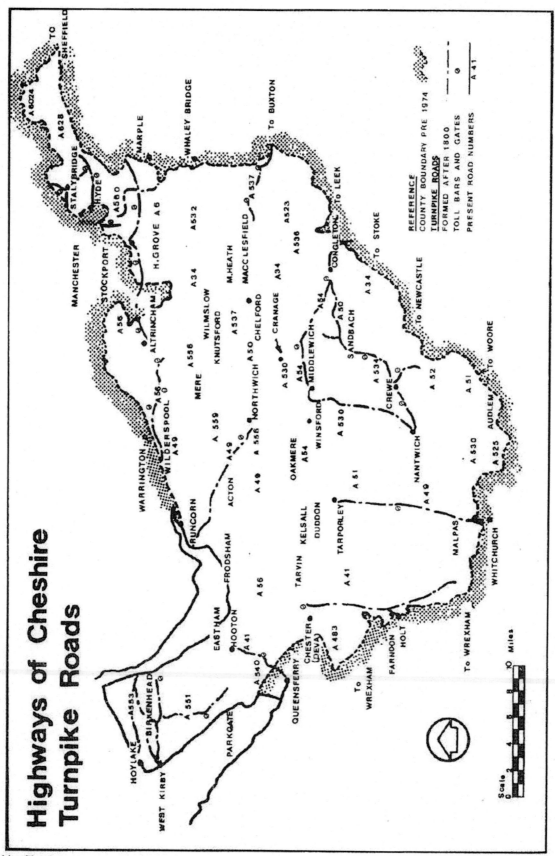

It would be surprising had there not been suspicion and doubts about this new scheme but the mounting pressure of increasing traffic on the main routes, plus the fact that turnpikes assisted and reduced the parishes' liability to repair the busiest routes, led to the demand for more turnpikes. It could be seen that the advantages of the system outweighed the disadvantages. Turnpike management, however, was not without its problems, and some instances of dishonesty. Thomas Finchett, Surveyor to the Chester-Whitchurch Trust, was dismissed after financial irregularities were discovered. Gradually the standard of the roads improved and this was due in some measure to pressure from the Post Office who, with their mail coaches, were among the greatest users of the Turnpikes, albeit on a non-payment basis, for the Royal mails always had free passage.

Notice was given in the Chester Courant, on Wednesday, 23rd. November, 1853, that an application was to be made to Parliament for the Chester, Farndon and Worthenbury Turnpike Road, which would commence in Boughton and pass in, through, or into the several parishes, townships and other places, one of which was Huntington, as can be seen on the previous page. Plans were deposited with the Parish Clerks of the respective parishes for all interested parties to examine. Shortly afterwards a printed notice to landowners and others followed, dated December 1852, from Barker and Hignett, Chester.[34]

These communications aroused interest and some concern on the part of landowners such as Thomas Hincks and led to a spate of correspondence. His letter of 11th November 1852[35] to his agent, Mr. H. I. Turner, was mainly concerned with the fact that certain of his lands had been given up to the neighbouring estate of Mr. Brock Wood in return for keeping the road in repair and that changes due to the Toll road would relieve Brock Wood of that obligation and that Hincks himself would lose out on compensation. A close scrutiny of the Turnpike Plan[36] reveals Mr. Brock Wood to have the greatest frontage to the proposed new road.

Mr. Turner was in agreement with this concern because, as he pointed out, the frontage of Hincks' 'Butterbach (sic) Lands may some day become very valuable'.[37] He

---

[34] Cheshire Record Office, ZD / Hincks /278
[35] Ibid. ZD / Hincks /204 to H/209
[36] Appendix 3
[37] Cheshire Record Office, ZD / Hincks /205

then carried on to discuss the new bridge planned for at the Butterbach which would be higher than the existing one and so would require considerable alteration to the entrances to Hincks' lands there. Turner, however, could see nothing injurious to Mr Hincks property holdings or interests in the proposed road and, in fact, considered that it would materially improve Hincks' Estate.

A lengthy correspondence ensued with much discussion of the points of interest and it was finally agreed that the Butterbach road frontage be returned to Mr Hincks and that any lands either taken for the road, or no longer required, should be negotiated for at fair valuation.[38] A certain amount of the correspondence was taken up with the proposed position of a Toll House. Mr Hincks was anxious that it should be placed beyond the extreme point of his Butterbach Land and that he should 'be secured from any undue liabilities in the event of the Tolls not proving sufficient to defray the expenses and repairs upon the New Road'.[39] He also requested that the Bill for the Turnpike Road should contain a clause that no Toll bar shall be placed nearer to Chester than one mile and a half from the terminus at the Whitchurch and Chester Road, a matter that required the sanction of Parliament.

The only drawbacks to his requests were Lord Redesdale's objection[40] to the clause 'prohibiting the taking toll within a mile and a quarter of Chester' and that, as originally

intended, the designated site for the Toll House was placed at the Rake and Pikle (sic) Public House at the junction with Saighton Lane 'on that part of the tongue of land No.38.[41] Unfortunately, as by necessity Toll Houses were built on the roadside, very few are still

---

[38] Cheshire Record Office, ZD / Hincks /207
[39] Ibid. ZD / Hincks /210, 211
[40] Ibid. ZD / Hincks /212
[41] Ibid. ZD / Hincks /276

standing today as most were demolished when the old Turnpike roads were widened to make way for the next generation of road traffic.

It appears that Mr Hincks gained much from his dealings with the Promoters of the Turnpike[42] as well as profiting by the better situation of his land after the Turnpike Road improvements. For the larger landed proprietor the turnpike, like enclosure, was 'a highly profitable investment in financial terms'.

The Turnpike Trusts became increasingly redundant but how important were they before the coming of railways? What did they contribute, if anything, towards economic development? On an everyday level, better roads made travel easier and so helped to break down regional isolation, which promoted economic and social changes. They also benefited the landed interests as the improved roads enhanced the competitive position of an area, thereby contributing to higher rents and, as can be deduced from the Hincks correspondence, open land adjacent to the road became ripe for villa development.[43]

As well as the gain to landowners, plus what must have been a great boon in the easement of local everyday use and mobility, there was a stimulus to business interests and also to local labour. This was not confined to the parochial locality but extended to the surrounding area, not least of which was the city of Chester, the county town and established centre for business and local government. A study of the accounts of the Chester to Whitchurch Turnpike Trust, a 'next door' area to Huntington and also the one with which the Chester, Farndon, Worthenbury Turnpike Trust eventually amalgamated in 1871, reveals bills paid for printing various notices to Surveyors, bills for Statute Duty, magistrates orders and the like to John Fletcher, Printer and Proprietor of the Chester Courant.[44] Some years later a bill for advertising in the Manchester Times and in the Midland Counties Herald was paid to Thomas Fletcher, Printer and Proprietor of what had become the Chester Chronicle, at Fletcher's Buildings, Bridge Street Row, Chester.[45] Another printer, T. Griffith, of Grosvenor-street, Chester, was also used for bills of meetings, annual statements, cards and

[42] Cheshire Record Office, ZD / Hincks /276
[43] Ibid. ZD / Hincks /284
[44] Ibid, TRT/2/31
[45] Ibid, TRT/7/9

various notices about cutting hedges, amongst other things.[46] It is from a printed notice[47] concerning various tolls for a number of gates and routes that we gain the information that Toll tickets were of different colours for different gates. It can be seen, without an in-depth study, that the Turnpike Trusts' stationery and advertising requirements alone must have brought a welcome increase of business.

Some of these bills or receipts were for yearly trade accounts showing a regularity of business trading and, one would assume, profit.[48] Others were for simple, everyday items such as a lock for the Boughton Gate[49] and draining pipes,[50] bringing to mind the day-to-day details and upheaval inevitable in such an enterprise as road building.

Further perusal of these records reveals requirements such as the breaking of tons of stone[51]; 'Leveling a Gravel pitt'[52]; yards and yards of paving and finding stones and sand[53]; plus bills for the mending of picks and staling of hammers.[54] New tines were fastened to old forks, pieces of metal to spades when they were worn down, and even washers and hooks were repaired. This is a reflection of an economy in which articles made of metal were not lightly discarded. Indeed, nothing was lightly discarded, for even the smallest tool was carefully husbanded.

There were, of course, payments for labour.[55] Furthermore, names of labourers match up with those of the local inhabitants in various records such as the census, so local labour also benefited.

Not surprisingly with such huge undertakings, there were claims for damage such as cutting through a field of wheat.[56] Complaints such as these together with other matters

---

[46] Cheshire Record Office, TRT/7/8
[47] Ibid, TRT/7/10b
[48] Ibid, TRT/1/23
[49] Ibid, TRT/1/15
[50] Ibid, TRT/1/47
[51] Ibid, TRT/1/6 et al
[52] Ibid, TRT/1/36
[53] Ibid, TRT/1/50
[54] Ibid, TRT/1/33 et al
[55] Ibid, TRT/1/38
[56] Ibid, TRT/1/57

needing to be attended to in order to placate or satisfy landowners must have added much to the work load and expense as well as to the administration.

There were, of course, overheads to be considered together with all the minutiae of business accounting. Salaries had to be provided, and handled, for the Clerk, Finchett-Maddock[57] and the Surveyor, William Goff.[58] Loans to the Trust had to be negotiated and recorded. Then there was interest to be paid on those loans. Payments ranged from £2. 6s. 0d per annum to the Churchwardens of Christleton up to payments of £50. 0s. 0d to the Blue School. A list of the owners of bonds[59] shows a range of sizes of loan and the extent of the debt carried by a Turnpike Trust. Further business deals were involved in the letting of Tolls by Auction. When these various aspects are considered there was a considerable amount of gain, or at least a stimulation of the economy, whether by salary or wages, by interest paid, or by company dealings, as well as the more obvious advantage of improved road conditions.

In 150 years the turnpike system in Cheshire had expanded to form a new and vital road system of nearly 552 miles which were eventually included in the 630 miles of trunk and principal roads which existed in Cheshire prior to Local Government re-organisation. Thus the turnpikes played a great part in the development of the excellent modern road infrastructure. Furthermore, although the contribution of the canals and, more importantly, the railways, to economic growth overshadowed that of the turnpikes, these roads were a significant factor for those 150 years, and without them the growth and population of Huntington would have been much slower.

The very late turnpike development in Huntington, at a time when the system elsewhere was declining, begs the question - why? This was a time when the Grosvenor estate was consolidating its landholding. There was also their cheese factory development. Furthermore, the great amount of building entered into on that estate at this time, requiring large amounts of building materials to be transported, could have profited from a greatly improved road structure. There could have been pressure and interest from that quarter?

---

[57] Cheshire Record Office, TRT/1/66 et al
[58] Ibid, TRT/1/46 et al
[59] Ibid, TRT/7/1

Unfortunately the Turnpike system did not prove to be a good business venture. Throughout the sixteen years of the Trust's functioning it carried a debt ranging from £5,385. 1s. 4d. to £8,734. 8s. 8d. ending, at the point of its amalgamation with the Chester-Whitchurch Trust, 1st July 1871, with a total debt of £5,600. 0s. 0d. This weight of debt carried on through the years of amalgamation until its termination, 1st November 1877. The amount of debt had, by this time, reduced to £1,706. 14s. 10d.

Turnpike Trusts in the English counties were never abolished by Act of Parliament. Instead their duties were gradually assumed by other authorities and the trusts were allowed to expire.

Landownership and Changes

Landowners had dominated the countryside for many generations. In the nineteenth century, the affluent landowners who, in the main, lived on their rents and left farming to their tenants, held about seventy per cent of all land. Land gave power and it was still a major economic resource. In 1851 agriculture was still the greatest single source of employment amounting to one-fifth of the working population.

However, although the big farmers of the nineteenth-century were mostly tenants, and held only a little over a tenth of the land, they were, nonetheless, men of wealth and enterprise. Frequently their ownership accounted for but a part of their holding because they often rented large acreages of additional land. The purchase of a farm represented a saving in rent of three or four per cent of the capital required, whereas good farming could produce ten per cent or more. It was far more profitable to put spare resources into buying new equipment or in extending the scale of their operations. Farmers, therefore, were content to be tenants, gaining a good return on their investment, and feeling perfectly secure under a good landlord.

The large tenant had considerable bargaining power. Smaller tenants, also, might expect to go on indefinitely, provided they cultivated the land reasonably and did not fall too far behind with their rents. Landlords and their agents preferred to leave good tenants undisturbed and allowed farms to pass from father to son, even to widows and daughters. It was a general policy to continue with the family of the old tenant in preference to introducing strangers. The main priority was to be a good tenant who took care of the land.

Estates in Cheshire were rarely single, concentrated holdings. It often happened, as in Huntington, that several important landowners held parts of the same township. Landowners also held lands in the same area which were separated by other owners' holdings.[60] It then follows that landowners and their agents were constantly on the look-out for lands and properties that would enlarge and consolidate their estates.

HENLAKE MEADOW – THE FINISHING TOUCH

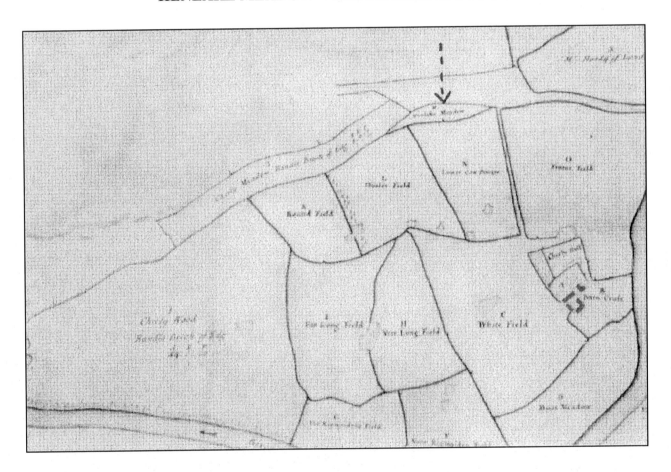

An Indenture made 13th. September, 1898, conveyed the Henlake Flash meadow, in the occupation of Frank Howell, from George Cooper of Huntington to Hugh Lupus, Duke of Westminster, together with two fee farm rents.[61] As can be seen from the plan, the ground in question appears as a missing piece of a jigsaw puzzle.

---

[60] Cheshire Record Office, ZD / Hincks / 228 & 235
[61] Grosvenor Estate Office Archives, Maps and Plans, Box R

This purchase would have been advantageous as it would have helped to enlarge and consolidate the Duke's land holding in that area. Furthermore, as the land was for estate consolidation the tenant would not be disturbed.

When John Hincks, however, desired to sell his property at Huntington and his agent had made approaches to Lord Westminster's agent in the hope of a sale, it took four months of negotiating before a deal was concluded.[62] This deal exemplifies the capabilities and worth of a good agent. Unlike the Henlake Flash sale, the proposed sale of Hincks property caused notice to be served on his tenant, Mr. Parker. Particular attention was paid as to the correct form of six clear months, as required by law.[63]

The agent was the most important person from a landowner's point of view. A good agent was not merely a representative of his employer but almost an alter ego, concerned with safeguarding the interests of the estate and of his employer as if they were his own. The position called for men of experience, probity and sound judgement for the agent had to negotiate and advise on property deals,[64] assess character when allocating tenancies, and decide whether a tenant who fell behind in his rent was the victim of misfortune or bad management. An agent needed knowledge of every kind of rural or farming undertaking. Furthermore, he had to be a thorough and regular correspondent as often the landowner visited or resided on other estates or, as in Captain Hincks case, resided abroad for health reasons.

Lawyers predominated for some time, partly because of the legal problems inherent in buying, selling and managing land. Towards the end of the nineteenth-century, however, particularly after the founding of the Institution of Surveyors in 1868, their place was taken by these professionally trained land agents.

Advancing agricultural methods were comparatively slow to reach the north-west of England but the rapidly rising industrial populations in Lancashire and north-east Cheshire,

---

[62] Cheshire Record Office, ZD / Hincks / 364-369
[63] Ibid. ZD / Hincks / 283
[64] Ibid. ZD / Hincks / 349

together with the food shortage due to the Napoleonic wars, stimulated production and resulted in the adoption of new methods in the early nineteenth century.

The land on the Cheshire plain had little natural drainage. Early attempts to get rid of the water were both expensive and inefficient. The invention of the circular tile and its support by Acts of Parliament in 1840, 1846 and 1850 was the big break-through. Thanks to a Government grant, tile manufacturers established themselves along the Chester and Ellesmere Canals and produced far more efficient tiles with their machinery. Many tile drains were laid in Cheshire and the drainage improved. Some landlords provided the tiles and the farmer provided the labour. Not all landlords were prepared to pay the whole cost of the tiles, though most of them seem to have been agreeable to pay some proportion.

By 1845 Cheshire farmers were aware of the advantages of draining with tiles, particularly on the heavy clay soil of the area. As little was understood of the theory and practice of drainage, in some cases, usually the smaller holdings, thousands of tiles were buried too deep or with insufficient fall. The commended practice, adopted on some of the large estates, was the laying of drains by skilled drainers under the supervision of the landlord's agent. This ensured more efficient work than could be expected from inexperienced farmers, who could then be charged two-thirds of the labour costs. The area of land drained increased 'one hundred fold' after the tile drainage.[65]

One of the biggest changes in farming was in the types of fertilizer used. Marling had gone on for centuries. The application of bone dust and chemical fertilizers, published in the farming journals, together with the use of older kinds of manure brought into the farm at a high cost of carriage, proved expensive. Added to which the use of the growing range of farm machinery was discouraged by the water-logged soils. Drainage, therefore, was seen as the essential pre-requisite of high farming. It was the first means by which the land was rendered capable of bearing richer crops and thus higher rents. Agents of the large estates were enthusiastic advocates of high farming, and, therefore, of drainage. Close attention to

[65] Davies, *Agricultural History of Cheshire, 1750-1850*, p. 71,

the efficient and precise overseeing by the agent of such work is clearly illustrated in the 1854 plans of work carried out on Mr. Hincks' land at Huntington.[66]

It then followed that farmers interested in practising the best modes of high farming wanted well-planned dairies, suitable housing for the efficient fattening of bullocks, farmyards designed to cope with manure and barns adapted to the use of steam power. Not surprisingly, this kind of farmer would not be satisfied with an inferior or inconvenient farmhouse. The landowner, therefore, was required to invest heavily in bricks and mortar. Again the agent's expertise was required for suitable designs and the supervision of construction.

Looking after the interests of the estate required constant and varied attention. If a suitable piece of land came on the market the agent moved swiftly to appraise it, inform his employer, and then forward the purchase. Similarly, he sold land for as good a price as possible.[67] During the Turnpike phase he studied the plans closely with the well-being of the estate in mind, and checked the progress and quality of work with a keen eye. During the landowner's continued absence he had to forward his views on the crops, their amount and their quality, plus the likely prices they should fetch. Attention had to be paid to the condition of the land and buildings and a full report and recommendation forwarded to the owner. [68]

The growth of large urban markets such as Liverpool, Manchester and the Potteries, and the expanding urban markets within the county in Wirral, together with the spread of the railways, led to a switching of milk from cheese making to the liquid milk market. The milk trade brought a regular return of cash, usually on a monthly basis, whereas cheese was sold in lots once or twice a year. The emphasis on dairy products, particularly the urban milk market, helped to shelter the Cheshire area from the severities of the 'Great Depression' that gripped much of British farming from 1873 to 1896. The large-scale urban demand in the industrial areas in the nineteenth century speeded the bias from subsistence to commercial agriculture and the farmer took his place as an important agent in the economic revolution.

---

[66] Cheshire Record Office, ZD / Hincks / 226 & 233
[67] Ibid, ZD / Hincks / 364-369
[68] Ibid, All correspondence in the Hincks Collection

Farming difficulties during the late nineteenth-century weighed heavily on many landowners, particularly those without another string to their bow. Industrial expansion and the slow march of democracy, added to agriculture's declining position in the country's economy, began to have an effect. Farming was no longer the centre of national life and the mainstay of a great proportion of the people. It was now only one among a number of major industries. Farming became part of the harsh world of commercialism.

Church Matters

The nineteenth century saw the growth of the Nonconformist movement, especially Wesleyan Methodists and the Primitive Methodists and resulted in the building of small chapels in many villages and even hamlets. The Primitives began their movement on the Cheshire-Staffordshire border under Hugh Bourne and William Clowes, who initiated the camp meetings on Mow Cop. The effects on public life were notable and the chapel-hamlet became a characteristic feature of the Cheshire countryside.

The Return to the Bishop's Inquiries before Visitation for Bruera Chapelry, made in 1804 by the vicar, the Reverend Thomas Maudsley,[69] stated there were four Methodist families and that they were 'shepherded' by Simon Ralphs, a local farmer and tenant of Sir Foster Cunliffe. The dissenters were said to attend meetings in Great Boughton at the home of 'Philip Oliver, Clerk', which building was licensed by the Bishop in 1793 for this purpose.[70] This cell had originated twenty years earlier, in 1784, when Philip Oliver arrived at Bruera as curate. On analysis, the only conclusion to the disparity displayed in these Returns is that the vicar at the time of the 1789 Return either had very little knowledge whatsoever of the parish and its daily life, or else he had deliberately avoided drawing attention to the matter, perhaps in the hope that it would 'die a natural death'.

An analytical approach to the entries in Peter Clubbe's memorandum in the 1839 Churchwardens' Account Book reveals that the need to provide a gallery for extra seating was

[69] Cheshire Record Office, MF / 44 / 10
[70] Ibid, EDA 13 / 2 / 147

during the ministry of the Reverend Oliver.[71] It is, therefore, reasonable to assume that he had radical tendencies when he was appointed and so generated, or encouraged, a growth of dissent in the parish. Furthermore, it is interesting to note the names of Joseph and Benjamin Clubbe, prominent local people, amongst those who supported his application for a licence,[72] which is some indication of the esteem in which he was held.

When the Reverend Maudsley made a Return in 1811, however, and he once more reported that there were no Papists in the parish, this time he did admit that dissent had grown and now included Independents and Presbyterians.[73] He added that there was still no place of worship for them in Bruera parish. A slight widening of the range of investigation, however, revealed the licensed meeting house of Daniel Ellis at Aldford,[74] which was but one mile away and an easier distance for those who had difficulty in travelling to Boughton.

There is further inconsistency in the 1821 Return, when the curate, the Reverend Marcie Domville-Taylor, denied that there was any non-conformity in the parish[75] but admitted, in the 1825 Return, that there was one meeting house in the parish.[76] Upon reflection, it is very likely that this was the Calvinist Methodist Chapel in the centre of Saighton village. The Ecclesiastical Census of 1851 shows that attendance in the chapel was considerable and rivalled that of the established church.[77]

Not surprisingly with such an old church, constant attention was required to maintain it. The extensive repairs, which included the replacement of roof timbers, slates, guttering and some masonry repairs, were paid for by raising a church rate among the parishioners. Out of the church rate for 1802-1803,[78] as well as the running repairs to the church fabric there were also many improvements made. In 1829 a long-needed vestry cost £3. 4s. 9d. followed in 1830 by a new, large window in the south wall "as the present one did not allow enough light to be shed on the pulpit".[79]

---

[71] Cheshire Record Office, Churchwarden's Account Book, 1839, P24 / 3
[72] Ibid, EDA 13 / 2 / 147
[73] Ibid, MF / /44 / 13 / 4 Bishops Inquiry before Visitation, 1811
[74] Ibid, EDA 13 / 2 / 164
[75] Ibid, MF 40 / 20 / 6, Bishops Inquiry before Visitation, 1821
[76] Ibid, MF 44 / 22 / 7, Bishops Inquiry before Visitation 1825
[77] Ibid, MF 11
[78] Ibid, P24 / 3
[79] Ibid, P24 / 3

In 1826, however, a problem arose when the Churchwardens of St. Oswald tried to impose a rate on Bruera to help towards paying for repairs to their church, which is St. Oswald, which had been ordered by the Bishop. Needless to say, the Churchwardens of Bruera felt that they had more than enough to contend with to maintain their own chapel without being expected to maintain the Mother Church as well. The returns to the Bishop's Inquiry before Visitation 1825[80] reveal that Bruera Chapel had to be supported entirely by the parishioners as there had been no land, bequests, or "monies" donated towards the upkeep of the main church fabric. The only exception to this was the chancel which was maintained by the minister and Sir Foster Cunliffe.

This injustice was felt so keenly that the churchwardens sought legal advice.[81] The advice they received was that they should resist these demands "at all costs" and to defend their right to independence in any court, civil or ecclesiastical and, should it be necessary, to raise a rate from time to time to meet the expense.[82] A committee was formed with this in mind[83] and the support of the landowners and occupiers of land in the area was solicited.[84]

The churchwardens then approached the Bishop for a ruling. They put forward the injustice of the situation whereby an under-populated parish such as that of Bruera, with persistently over-stretched resources in the struggle to maintain its own chapel, could, or should, be expected to assist in the maintenance of a church in a more populated and wealthy parish. It was further pressed that Bruera had become independent of St. Oswald's in the past and, therefore, was not liable anyway.

This latter fact was confirmed some days later by Mr. Ward, the Diocesan Registrar, after he had discovered an important document relating to the case in the archives. He provided a copy for the churchwardens to place in the parish chest. This document was the resulting decision of a trial held in 1712,[85] first at Chester and then later, on appeal, to York,

[80] Cheshire Record Office, MF 44 / 22
[81] Ibid. ZD / Hincks / 374
[82] Ibid. ZD / Hincks / 332
[83] Ibid. ZD / Hincks / 332, 371, 374
[84] Ibid. ZD / Hincks / 373
[85] Ibid, DDX 448 / 6

where it was recorded that Bruera was completely independent and had since been nominating its own vicar.

Although St. Mary's, Bruera, was accepted as being independent of St. Oswald's, it was still under the patronage of the Dean and Chapter of Chester Cathedral. The fact that the patrons could nominate a vicar by "direct instrument" did not alter the situation for the parish was still annexed to St. Oswald's and so the status quo remained whereby the Vicar of St. Oswald's was automatically the Vicar of Bruera.

Encouraged by their success on this point, together with the document of proof from the 1712 trial, however, the churchwardens of Bruera wrote once more to the Bishop and to the Ecclesiastical Commissioners on the 17th. October 1861[86] asking to be allowed their own resident vicar. They pointed out that under the present arrangements their vicar was always absent. He supplied a curate, at his own expense, to attend to the parish.[87] It was further pointed out that Bruera possessed nearly twenty acres of glebe land on which a vicarage could be built "which could surely be paid for out of the monies that the church had recently from the sale of property in the area". [88] It was all to no avail and there was no alteration in the system until 1868.

That Bruera appears to have been of minor importance to most of the curates, and their superiors, is demonstrated by the fact that the cure was held in addition to other posts in the church. As an example, the curate in 1778, James Whinfield, lived in Chester which was five miles away, added to which he also held a position in "little St. Mary's within the Cathedral".[89] This required him to take daily prayers in that church, for a stipend of twelve pounds per annum. Such a requirement would make it extremely difficult for him to provide a proper service to the parishioners in the outlying parish of Bruera at a distance of five miles.

The many appointments to the position of curate reflect a lack of interest in Bruera parish on the part of the Cathedral officials, the Chester-based Vicars of St. Oswald and the Bishop. The Cathedral dignitaries must have been aware of the unsatisfactory nature of the

---

[86] Cheshire Record Office, DDX 448 / 1-6
[87] Ibid, EDP 51 / 1 / 1
[88] Ibid. DDX 448 / 1-6
[89] Ibid, MF / 44 / 1 Bishops Inquiry before Visitation 1778

situation for each time a curate was appointed the Vicar of St. Oswald's informed the Lord Bishop.[90]

The chapelry, including the four townships of Churton Heath, Lea Newbold, Saighton and Huntington, was formed into a separate parish in 1868 when Thomas Bell was appointed the first vicar.

Whether there was resentment on the part of the Cathedral authorities because of Bruera's stand cannot be stated.   Nevertheless their total lack of consultation, or consideration, when they ignored the Churchwardens' request to appoint the Curate of Bruera as the first resident Rector,[91] and passed him by in favour of another cleric, Thomas Bell, appears overbearing and unchristian in the extreme. It does appear to underline the great gap in understanding and total lack of consultation between those in authority and those 'beneath them'.

The system whereby those who had the means could buy their seat in church is illustrated in the Churchwardens' accounts for 1839. A gallery was built to provide thirty extra seats in the church and a handrail for the *Galery stairs* cost five shillings. A memorandum was written by Peter Clubbe, a local landowner and churchwarden, to show how the seats in the new gallery had been allocated. The project had been funded by selling the seats with the dearest ones at the front.[92]   Mr. Richard Dutton, the senior churchwarden, had been given the task of organizing the finance as well as supervising the construction work and in recognition of this he was given first choice of the seats. Not surprisingly, nor unnaturally, he took the first row.

The need for the memorandum becomes clear upon reading the rota of events following the deaths of Mr Dutton and his wife when the seats became vacant. As Peter Clubbe was Richard Dutton's uncle and the nearest surviving relative he took over the front row seats and so allowed Mary Colley, owner of Churton Heath estate, to move from the third row to his second row. In 1841, however, when Mary Colley left the area and John Ralphs

---

[90] Cheshire Record Office, EDP 51 / 1 / 1
[91] Ibid. P24 / 3 193 / 9
[92] Ibid, P24 / 3, Churchwardens' Account Book, 1839

took over as tenant of the estate, he was required to move back to the original seat. Obviously there were strict rules of precedence and the gradations of status had to be upheld. Mr Clubbe concluded by saying that the two back rows of seats were free of payment and were reserved for the poor of the parish. In 1877 it was announced that in future all seats in the church were to be free of all "rent and charge". People, however, continued to keep to their old seats as is shown by Miss Denton of Newbold being allowed to put a door on 'her' pew at the rear of the church.[93]

R.W. Boden, Esquire, writing of the old church in the magazine of 1907, states that the "seats of oak were arranged as boxed-in pews, with doors and fasteners. A small sloping gallery was at one time occupied by the church orchestra and schoolchildren".[94] This mention of a church orchestra fits in with the mention in the Churchwardens Account book for 1818-19 of the need for new 'strings for viol - 10/6d'.[95] It also coincides with the assessment for church rates of Mr Thomas Tilston of Lea Newbold[96] from which it appears that he was both orchestra leader and instrument repairer. The addition of cellos in 1819, as per a bill of 15s/8d to Thos. Eaton for strings for violincello, and of clarinets in 1842 (Clarionet Reads 1/-) suggests that under his guidance the orchestra thrived and expanded. It continued to do so until 1847 as 'Claronet Reads & Violin strings cost 6/-.' At some point afterwards music was provided by a harmonium for in 1860 a reference is made to its removal to another place in the church in the entry 'Jos. Swindley for moving organ etc. - 2/-, together with the cost of 'binding music book' - 1/6d' [97]

As the centre of population was being shifted to Saighton village due to the expansion of the Grosvenor Estate, the Bishop of Chester granted a licence for the performance of Divine Service in the School Room at Saighton.[98] At the same time, due to the continuing deterioration of the Bruera church fabric, together with this population shift, a plan was mooted to erect a new parish church in Saighton.[99] This, however, did not come to pass but an offer was made by the Duke of Westminster for a complete restoration of Bruera's church,

---

[93] Cheshire Record Office, Churchwardens' Account Book, 1900
[94] R. Richards, Old Cheshire Churches, p.72, footnote 1.
[95] Cheshire Record Office, P24 / 3, Churchwardens' Account Book, 1818-19
[96] Ibid, QDV 2 / 248, Land Tax assessments for Lea Newbold
[97] Ibid, P 24 / 3, Churchwardens' Account Books, 1819-1860
[98] Ibid, EDP 51 / 4
[99] Ibid, Kelly's Directory of Cheshire 1892

which was accepted. Raymond Richards says *the 1896 restoration was in effect a wanton and unnecessarily severe rebuilding of much of the church.*[100] In Bruera, however, on 21st July 1896, a meeting of the parishioners was held in Saighton School to thank the Duke for giving them such a beautiful building.[101]

School Development

The information contained in the 1804 Return from Bruera[102] to the Bishop's Inquiries before Visitation states that the only school is a flourishing Methodist Sunday School of about twenty children which was held in the house of Simon Ralphs and had been so "for the last twenty years". There appears to be no information, however, that this was a licensed meeting house for dissenters. The confusion and fluctuation in information carries on through to the 1811 Return[103] in which it was reported that there were two small day schools with about twenty pupils in each.

NEW SCHOOL SPECIFICATION

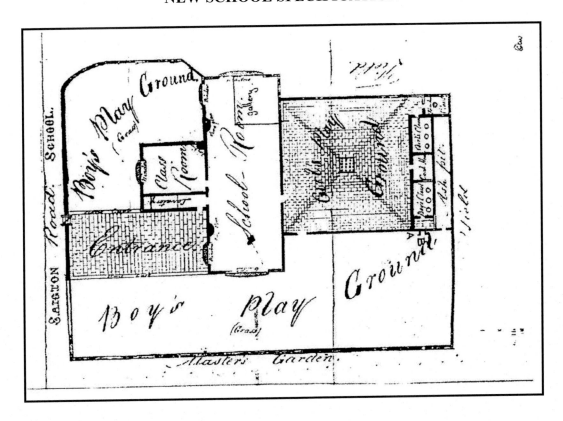

[100] Richards, R., *Cheshire Churches*, p. 70
[101] Cheshire Record Office, SL 122 / 1 Saighton School Log Book
[102] Ibid, MF 44 / 16 Bishops Inquiry, 1804
[103] Ibid, MF 44/13 Bishops Inquiry, 1811

Ormerod states that a Sunday school was erected about 1830, adjacent to the church, built and maintained by voluntary subscription, and giving his source as Dr. Denton of Newbold.[104]   There is no archival support, however, for this. The building is described in White's Directory of 1860 as a small brick structure built to house seventy children and Ann Formston is named as the mistress. She appears in the 1851 Census as School Mistress and also that she was born in Shropshire. Her husband, John Formston, is named as School Assistant and he was born in Aldersey, so it is reasonable to assume she came some time earlier as School Mistress and that they subsequently married. Her husband left his trade as a shoemaker to act as her assistant, although he had reverted back to that trade by 1861. Religious instruction played a prominent part in the teaching, and in most schools this, with the 3Rs, was all that was offered. There is no information regarding the governing body of the school at this period.

In spite of the apparent contradictions in the ecclesiastical documentary evidence it seems clear that the school did exist and its position next to the church is confirmed on the Tithe Map for Saighton.[105]   It continued in use until it was replaced in 1862/3 by the new school provided by the Duke of Westminster in Saighton village. The continued demolition of houses around the village of Bruera and relocation of the population in either Saighton or Aldford, due to the expansion of the Grosvenor Estate, made this move inevitable.

The specification for the new school, found in Appendix 4[106] illustrates the quality of work expected by the Duke of Westminster from those working on his behalf. It goes into precise detail for all the trades involved and specifies from whom certain materials are to be obtained. Even so, changing ideas and requirements, amongst which was a rapid increase in the numbers of children, called for alterations and additions throughout the rest of the century. It was intended, from the beginning that the school should meet all the needs of the community, whether social, religious or educational. The building consisted of a main schoolroom, with a gallery at one end, and one small classroom.[107]

---

[104] Ormerod, G. *The History of the County Palatine and City of Chester, Ed.2, revised T. Helsby* (London), p. 763
[105] Cheshire Record Office, EDT 349 / 2
[106] Ibid, P 24 / 4   Specification for Saighton School
[107] Plan of Saighton School, courtesy of Gordon Watkinson

It appears that Ann Formston moved with the school into the new building in Saighton village as she is still confirmed in the 1871 Census as School Mistress, with her nineteen-year old son, Ernest, as Assistant. Again it is not clear just who the overall authority was at this stage. In all likelihood it was the church, for in 1868 reference is made to a cleaner being appointed for the 'new' school and that her wages were to be paid by the vestry.[108] Unfortunately no log book record of Ann Formston's headship survives.

The first page of the log book[109] for this school under new headship opens with 'Mr and Mrs Lloyd commenced duties at Saighton National School, 1st January 1872.' (The school's name is an indication that it had been taken into the public elementary system set up by the 1870 Forster Education Act). 'Number of children on Books, 49. Reverend D. Shaw opened Schools. Master gave a lesson in the presence of the Vicar, subject: - Notation and Numeration'. It goes on to say, 'Examined the whole School in Reading, Writing and Arithmetic, in a very miserable condition, only one out of 48 passed in Standard I'. The Inspector's report of March 1872 mentions a 'good start being made by the new school' which appears to be a confirmation that the school had been in use since 1862-3.

These twice-yearly examinations were of great importance for on the results might depend the master's reputation and salary. On them, too, rested the question of which children would be allowed to leave school at eleven or twelve, which was a matter of large concern to their parents. Compulsory education, introduced in the decade after 1870, meant that children's earnings, no matter how meagre, were curtailed and so were sorely missed by poor parents who often resented the undue burden of school attendance. Added to this burden, before the abolition of school fees in 1891, was the weekly charge of a few pence a week for schooling. This was especially serious where there were several children of school age.

The low standards which the Lloyds reported finding upon their arrival rapidly improved and the numbers of pupils also increased rapidly. The Lloyds were aided in the teaching by the vicar, Reverend Shaw, who taught Scripture, and his sister, who taught

---

[108] Cheshire Record Office, P 24 / 4
[109] Ibid, SL 122 / 1

sewing. Hardly a day went by without the Vicar opening school and conducting Scripture lessons. Local gentry and their ladies, as well as Lord Westminster, visited the school. The ladies inspected the needlework and heard the children sing. School Inspectors on their annual inspections praised the Lloyds highly for what they had accomplished.

Although some parents believed in education as a means to advancement, poor attendance was a problem for teachers. The boys would be employed helping their fathers or the farmers at busy seasons. Girls were kept at home to mind yet another baby or help finish some piece of work to bring some money in. Work, however, was not the only reason for absenteeism. Lack of sound footwear in bad weather or being unable to get boots on because their feet were sore with chilblains could prevent their attendance. Furthermore, parents might need a week or two to find money for new shoes.

Education was seen as a means of instilling habits of responsibility, sobriety, obedience, respect for authority and frugality among the poor. Great emphasis was placed on Religious Education and Scripture lessons were given every day. As well as the Bible and the Catechism, they included homilies on not lying, or stealing, or being discontented or envious. They must accept that God had placed them in their position in life and it would be sinful to wish otherwise. The overriding purpose was to train the children in the ways of honest and reliable service and to know 'their place'.

Then, at their peak in numbers of pupils, something seems to have gone wrong, for in 1880 the HM Inspector's report speaks for the first time of slipping standards and bad record keeping. This could have been due to the pressure of teaching over a hundred children in the small school. There is, however, an entry for 2nd. March, 1877, which says, 'Master received the last Quarter Salary from the managers who deducted, by the order of The Eaton Estate Office, the Superannuation Fee of five pounds, three shillings and eight pence, which had formerly been allowed the master'. Might this have caused a feeling of not being appreciated and so added a (further) despondency to the teaching difficulties? Whatever the reason, January 1881 saw a new teaching staff at Saighton.

Thomas and Jane Barker, father and daughter, took charge and gave a very critical report of the state of everything, with poor performances, poor attendance and bad or nonexistent records. It was not long, however, before the Barkers began to see results, with increasing numbers and better performances. The 1883 HM Inspector's report suggested that extra staff should be employed to help the Barkers, and so Anne Dutton was employed as a stipendiary monitor, a position which was retained on the school staff for many years. This position carried a salary of £20 per annum, compared with £30 per annum for the mistress and £120 for the master, and was filled by some local girls, Elizabeth Astle in 1890, and a Miss Jones until at least 1902.

1886 saw some changes. The Reverend Shaw moved to Alsager and so Mr. Barker lost both his help and that of his sister, Miss Shaw. Moreover, the new vicar, the Reverend Dunn, did not involve himself with the school to the same degree. Jane Barker also left at the same time and her place was taken by her mother.

The school was declared "free" under the Free Education Act of 1891. Its administration then remained unaltered until the abolition of the voluntary schools system in 1903.

It was previously mentioned that the new school was built to serve all the needs of the community and so in 1867 the Bishop licensed the building to be used "for the convenience of the people of the village" for baptisms and communion services.[110] All chapel services and eventually all vestry meetings were held in the school. During the winter months the school was used as an entertainments centre, for producing shows themselves and also bringing in outside entertainers, and people to give lectures. The organization of such events owed much to Lady Grosvenor, as did all aspects of village life.

The young men of the village were allowed to use the infants' classroom also during the winter months as a smoking/reading room but unfortunately this, together with all outside uses, led to friction and accusations of breakages. Matters were brought to a head one morning in 1896 when the Schools Inspector discovered that "the air was foul and the place was left in a very dirty state", following its use by the young men the previous night. Action as then taken to amend the situation. The school was also used as a centre for rent collection on quarter days for the Eaton Estate.

---

[110] Cheshire Record Office, EDA Bishops Act Book & EDP 51 / 4 Licence

The school was also involved in the annual club wake, which appears to have been a procession from farm to farm and included stops for refreshment, when the walkers usually arrived back at the school somewhat tired and unsteady for lunch. This was followed by games and dancing on the school cricket field until well into the night. A sad incident in connection with these festivities is recorded in the school's log book: - "Benjamin DUTTON, aged 8 years, Standard II, died on Sunday afternoon, June 14th. 1874, after five days illness, caused by taking to excess intoxicating drink at the Village Club, June 9th." In this case, at least, the homilies on sobriety and obedience do not appear to have borne fruit.

For a school to thrive before the national system came into being it was almost essential that some individual/s made it their special interest. The success of Saighton School obviously owed much to the keen interest of the Grosvenor family for they not only provided the parish with the school in the first place, but maintained it and developed it as the years passed by. The Grosvenors always took their role as school governors very seriously, as is illustrated by this extract from the log book: - "Dismissed - Eliza PLEAVIN, for violating Lord Westminster's third rule" – 9th May 1873. There is no record of what Lord Westminster's third rule was or, indeed, his first and second rules. It is likely that they were concerned with punctuality, hands and faces washed, hair cut short and combed, clothes as neat as possible, respect for teachers, care of slates and books, diligence, reverence at prayers, and to be truthful and honest.

The Grosvenors took a continuing active interest in everything to do with the school with frequent family visits to see for themselves the progress that was being made there. The 1896 report of the HM Inspector which stated that Saighton School, "was altogether a very good example of the very best of country schools"[111] this must have been a source of pleasure to them. Their interest was not confined to the children's education but extended to the physical and material needs of the children. This was accomplished in many ways, from periodically providing clothes for them, to giving them and their mothers an annual "treat" on the lawns of the Towers, which the Duke, the Duchess and Lady Grosvenor always attended.

Other local dignitaries shared in this interest and involvement as is illustrated by the number of visits made to the school together with the provision of various "treats" at

---

[111] Cheshire Record Office, SL 122 / 1 Saighton School Log Book, p. 386

Newbold, Golbourn Hall and Saighton Hall. The children were expected and encouraged to join in the many Eaton Estate organized events, such as the annual Eaton music festival. Whenever important visitors came to visit Eaton Hall the children were invited to welcome them, as was the case on the occasions when the Prince of Wales came to stay with the Grosvenors. Although this was undoubtedly meant kindly it was, however unwittingly, an underlying reinforcement of the respectful, grateful and obedient attitude expected from the 'deserving poor' that was so prevalent at that time.

Nineteenth-century developments based on the census and trade

Huntington was never a village in the accepted sense, with a variety of buildings around the church, but an area, or hamlet, of scattered farmsteads and cottages. As a certain minimum size of population was needed to support a particular craft or trade, and also because of Huntington's particular involvement with the other outlying townships of Saighton and Bruera, a group analysis of the three townships will provide a better illustration of how these nineteenth century developments affected occupations and trade in the area. Indeed, to ignore the Grosvenor interest in Saighton, and the resulting expansion particularly, would be to miss a large portion.

A study of the statistics contained in the census returns of 1851-1891 reveals the change from a purely agricultural economy to one more diversified and relating to the industrial advances and commercial interest. During the course of the nineteenth century the situation changed from that where the majority of the population was employed as either agricultural labourers or servants, with only a sprinkling of trades' people, to one where this predominance waned as the century progressed.

It must be pointed out that the census record of 1891 for Saighton appears to lack eighteen dwellings and their families. Whether this is due to inefficiency on the enumerator's part, or maybe some other problem, cannot be ascertained. Cheshire County Record Office has been informed but no solution has presented itself as yet. For the purposes of this analysis, however, it is not an insurmountable problem. Indeed, the problems due to human error and difficulties with bad handwriting are integral to the study of archives.

The growth of industrialisation in Britain affected farming deeply. Added to this was the competition from imports of cheaper foodstuffs. It became necessary for farmers to adopt a more commercial, more technical, more capital-intensive system of soil cultivation. Nor were they the only ones to be affected by the changes. The coming of the turnpike roads had opened up many isolated places and the easing of travel and communication meant that there was more contact with outside ideas and knowledge of other choices of occupation and easier daily lives.

Important changes such as the coming of compulsory education after 1870 and the extension of the franchise, together with the Secret Ballot, brought a wind of change and gradually contributed to higher expectations. Furthermore, the activity of industrial unions with their self-educated men, some of them Non-conformist lay preachers, together with the advent of the railways, visits to towns, newspapers and the penny post, all tended to draw the rural worker into the current of contemporary life.

Drainage was seen to be the foundation of greater efficiency and the means whereby the land was to be enabled to bear richer harvests, of itself desirable, and also to lead to higher rents. The invention of the circular tile, together with Government support, was a big break through. Tile making businesses were established and a new source of employment appeared. Drainage operations created a great deal of work. One million tiles per year were

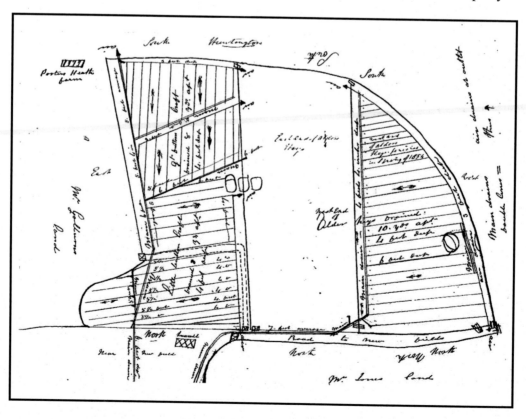

being used in the 1840s on the Duke of Westminster's estates in the Broxton Hundred and ninety miles of drains had been constructed to drain 500 acres.[112]

A brick and tile labourer, a caster, (very likely a tile caster), bricklayers, brick makers and a stone mason are to be found in the 1851 census for Saighton and the 1861 for Huntington. Drainage operations provided even more work when landowners thought it good business sense to match the newly-drained fields with new barns, dairies, cow pens and pigsties.

Once the holding of the Grosvenor estate in the area had been increased, the Marquis of Westminster's massive rebuilding programme in the second half of the century created many more chances for skilled work. Initially most of the skilled labour had to be imported for the building work but this provided opportunities for apprenticeships for local boys together with allied labouring work for the men. The reconstruction of farms and cottages, the building of the new school, and the rebuilding of the church at Bruera, created a great demand for bricks and other building materials, thus leading to an increase in trade and created a local demand for the skills needed for their manufacture which, in turn, led to further job opportunities. Property repairs for the Grosvenor Estate kept ironmongers, carpenters, sawyers, masons and painters in constant employment. Carters were kept busy carting bricks.

Platts Rough is revealed as the site of the brickworks and also part of the Grosvenor Estate in the specification of the proposed new school for Saighton. The Ennion family took over the running of the works, eventually installing steam power to boost production. This business was run down in the 1890s when new brickmaking sites were opened on other parts of the Grosvenor Eaton Estates.

Walter Bodin, Diocesan Architect, appears as a resident of Saighton in the census return of 1871. This may have been due to a desire, or a need, to be available for consultation with the Duke of Westminster. It illustrates the developing trend away from the Agents, who had acted for so long in a multiple overseeing capacity, and towards the specialist

---

[112] Davies, *Agricultural History of Cheshire, 1750-1850*, p. 109

professionals. Or it might be that while he was supervising the refurbishment of Bruera Church he was attracted to the locality. He was joined by his son in 1891, also as an Architect. A further illustration of the rapidly changing developments of the nineteenth century is provided by the 1891 census record for Saighton of farmer's son, William Allwood, as a mechanical engineer and draughtsman.

Although the loss of houses in Bruera, due to the development of Saighton as a centre because of the expansion of the Grosvenor Estate, is shown as a drop backwards to one farm and eleven inhabitants, in 1871, it was not a move backwards to total rural isolation and outlook. The new trend in employment and readiness to grasp the new commercial opportunities is apparent as the farmer's son is recorded to be a Draper.

The Duke of Westminster's cheese factory at Aldford created further jobs and the opportunity to ascend the employment ladder, from ordinary worker to Cheese Factor. William Taylor is recorded as a Cheese Factor in the 1881 census return. It was also a move from individual cheese-making in the various farmhouses to commercial production.

The coming of the turnpike road provided work for a toll gate keeper in Huntington. It provided better access to local markets for the farmers even though the many tolls constituted an extra charge. This road improvement which did so much for easier communication is evident in the increasing number of carters from 1861 onwards and also indicates a great increase in carriage work and an expansion of trade.

In spite of fears to the contrary, the advent of the railways also brought increased work for the carters. Rail passengers had to be brought to the railway station and then delivered home again. It was also the railways that opened up the rapidly expanding urban populations and enabled the switch from cheese production to milk distribution which was not only an expansion and a strengthening of the farming economy but greatly improved the farmers' cash flow. Instead of having to rely on an annual or bi-annual cheese payment to support credit, the milk cheques 'flowed' monthly. Census returns from 1861 onwards record a variety of new jobs in connection with the railways, which include a carter at the railway, a railway policemen, a railway labourer, a railway porter and platelayers.

Some country businesses, however, expanded with the changing times. Enterprising carpenters and blacksmiths sometimes developed into specialized manufacturers of agricultural implements. The 1881 census return for Saighton records Charles Palin as a blacksmith employing two men and two boys. He appears to have had a thriving business.

There was an increasing trend for daughters to become dressmakers or, as in the case of Elizabeth Phoenix of Huntington, a milliner, instead of going out in service. Many sons no longer followed their fathers automatically onto farms. The agricultural labourers could see the advantages of being tradesmen and so apprenticed their sons to tradesmen for the first time, which helped to build up a reservoir of skill.

Daniel Woodcock of Huntington is recorded in the census return of 1871 for Huntington as a Corn Factor's assistant and John Pleavin of Saighton as a Cooper. Gardeners appear towards the end of the century.

Instead of home brewing, the beer house, or public house, emerged. Ann Morgan, the enterprising wife of an agricultural labourer, branched out as a Barm and Ginger Beer Manufacturer in the census return of 1871 for Saighton and Margaret Medcock, wife of a stone mason, was a shopkeeper.

By 1881 a grocer's shop had appeared in Saighton, followed by another one in 1891. The appearance of shops was associated with the spread into consumption of such former luxuries as tea, coffee and sugar, but they also stocked a wide range of non-perishable foodstuffs and household. Prior to this the local population had lived pretty much off their own produce. The labourers, who in any case had a very simple diet, often got their milk, cheese, bacon and corn from the farms.

The provision of the 'Penny Post' as a national service was another great development. As the postmaster recorded in the 1891 census return for Saighton was not a local man, doubtless his appointment was due to previous experience in Post Office work. The entry for Saighton in the Kelly's Directory of 1896, however, reveals a local man, Samuel Pleavin, as shopkeeper and sub-postmaster of the Post Office. Letters were handled here and postal orders issued, but no money was paid out.

This was one break with the close connection Huntington had with Saighton. Huntington's letters came through Chester and the nearest money order office was at Boughton-in-the-City. This 'separation' of affairs was to continue. In this respect, it could be said that the nineteenth century changes which brought new occupations and new outlooks and left so much of the old ways behind, were the start of a gradual 'weaning' of Huntington from its old ties with Saighton and Bruera.

It must be understood, however, that the Huntington of the nineteenth century as recorded in the censuses of 1841 to 1891 was very much that of the present day rural half. In spite of the changes it was still a farming area, and indeed still is. It is the change to working farmer occupiers, as opposed to landowners and their tenant farmers that is the relevant factor. In other words, the dichotomy of Huntington has to be kept in mind.

The census returns for the populations of Huntington and Cheaveley, Saighton and Bruera are respectively:[113]

Population Returns for Huntington and Cheaveley, Saighton and Bruera								
	1801	**1811**	**1821**	**1831**	**1841**	**1851**	**1861**	**1871**
Huntington	111	124	133	112	143	129	113	119
Saighton	242	247	291	303	313	329	272	309
Churton Heath	8	7	8	14	3	22	44	11

	1881	**1891**	**1901**	**1911**	**1921**	**1931**	**1951**	**1961**	**1971**
Huntington	120	110	121	117	126	144	2614	1603	1273
Saighton	344	362	308	327	362	347	312	308	245
Churton Heath	8	7	7	16	7	15	15	18	16

By 1998 the figure given for the population of Huntington and Cheaveley by Cheshire County Council was 2100. It will be noted that the great increase in population is only marked in 1951, well after the 1930s building development and the ensuing migration, because there was no census in 1941 due to the war. The numbers for Saighton and Churton

---

[113] *Victoria History of the County of Chester, Vol.II,* pp. 212, 218, 229

Heath have remained fairly constant. These figures further underline the changes that came about in Huntington due to the change in landownership which will be explored in the next chapter.

FOREWORD

A few particulars regarding the well built houses now being erected at Huntington on the Butter Bache Estate.

The Estate is beautifully situated on the banks of the River Dee, on a height commanding wonderful views of the city and its Cathedral, and surrounded by many acres of open land which can never be built upon. Some of the houses now being built will have an uninterrupted view stretching away for many miles.

The Estate is exactly 1½ miles from Chester Cross, on the main road to Farndon, and overlooks the beautiful stretch of river leading to Herons Bridge.

The Estate is served by two Chester Corporation Bus services, one to the Red House Hotel, at one end of the Estate, and the other to the Rake & Pikel Inn beyond the Estate, while the Crossville service is also available.

3

GENERAL INFORMATION

Water.	Supplied by Chester Waterworks Co., Newgate St., Chester. The supply is constant and liberal and of exceptional purity.
Sewer.	A new main sewer has been specially constructed by the Chester R.D.C. to serve this Estate.
Gas.	Gas is supplied by the Chester United Gas Co., Northgate Street, Chester, at charges of 8d. per therm. or 3.2 per 1,000 cu. ft.
Electricity.	Electricity is supplied by the Chester Corporation. Showrooms, Northgate Street. Domestic Tariff 12½% on nett rateable value plus 6d. per unit. Lighting Tariff 4.4d. per 1st 1,000 K.W.'s.
Rates.	The Rating authority is the Chester Rural District Council. The rates for the district are 10/1 in the £.
Shopping Facilities.	A shopping centre has been incorporated in the lay-out of the Estate and is most centrally situated.
Church.	A large piece of land in the centre of the Estate has been freely given to the Ecclesiastical Authorities for the erection of a Church, and a Mission Hall is now being erected, under the active leadership of the Rev. H. N. Doig, Vicar of the Parish.

4

Type "A" Semi-Detached Bungalows

The bungalows stand back 23ft. from the front boundary, the complete depth of the plots being from 150ft. to 200ft. thereby giving spacious gardens at the rear.

Most of the back gardens are bounded by a beautiful wood overlooking the river, the remainder having a wonderful open country outlook.

ACCOMMODATION.   **Extremely large principal entertaining Room** with Bay Window and tiled fireplace with raised tiled hearth. Electric power plugs.

Cosy living Room on sunny side with tiled fireplace and raised hearth. Fitted wireless plug.

Three Bedrooms. Two fitted with electric power plugs.

Tiled Bathroom with 5ft. 6in. Bath. W.C.

Pantry conveniently placed to Living Room and Scullery.

Scullery with ample shelf accommodation and all-white sink.

5

Type "B" Semi-Detached Houses

The houses stand back 23ft. from the front boundary, the complete depth of the plots being from 150ft. to 200ft., thereby giving spacious gardens at the rear.

There is room for a garage and double gates are provided.

ACCOMMODATION.   **Large Front Entertaining Room** with Bay Window and tiled fireplace with raised hearth.

Large Living Room overlooking back garden with extra large windows.

Hall with panelled staircase.

Scullery complete with gas boiler, white sink and ample shelves.

Pantry with cold slab.

Bathroom, white tiled and fitted with 5ft. 6in. Bath. W.C.

Large Front Bedroom with bay window and fitted with electric power plug.

Large Bedroom overlooking back garden also fitted with electric power plug.

Small Bedroom of ample size.

6

CHAPTER SIX

The Twentieth Century Developments

A study of the Valuation Lists for the Parish of Huntington for 1898 - 1908[114] shows the land to be in the holding of two major landowners, the Duke of Westminster and George Cooper, Esquire. A smaller holding was in the ownership of Dr. Denton and John Jones is shown as an owner-occupier. Although the Valuation Lists for 1909 to 1912 show several minor discrepancies they are of no importance. The list of major landowners remained constant.

VALUATION LIST 1898 - 1908

Number	NAME OF OCCUPIER.	NAME OF OWNER.	Description of Property.
1	Alitt Hannah	George Cooper	Farm
2	Walley R. T.	Duke of Westminster	do
3	Salmon Thomas	do	do
4	Alfred Joseph	George Cooper	do
5	Hewitt John	do	do
6	Howell F	do	do
7	Jones John	Self	do
8	Parkington B	Duke of Westminster	do
9	Hewitt John	Dr. Denton	Land
10	Parks Thomas	do	do
11	Winshull John	Duke of Westminster	do
12	Brown Bob	George Cooper	Farm
13	Howell W.	do	do
14	Phenix H.	Dr. Denton	Land
15	do	George Cooper	Public Ho., Bldgs & Land
16	Jones Robert	Duke of Westminster	Farm
17	Salisbury Joseph	do	do
18	Lloyd Ann	George Cooper	do
19	Hughson William	do	do
20	Evans Elizabeth	C. J. Hinerks	Land
21	Salisbury Joseph Senr	George Cooper	House & do
22	Smith Bob	do	do
23	Tilston W.	do	do
24	Reptd of J. Parry	Selves	Land

---

114 Cheshire Record Office, RGT / 64

It is in the Valuation Lists of 1920 that the changes in landowning become apparent. This, not surprisingly, illustrates the effects of the later-mentioned sale of the Huntington Estate. The Duke of Westminster still figures but the preponderance of a small number of major estate holders has changed. There are still some lands in the hands of the Cooper Trustees but the rest are either owner-occupiers or small owners renting out. A shift of power from traditional landowner to local government authority is displayed. Cheshire County Council appears as owner of two houses or buildings which are occupied by a Thomas Morgan and George Grace. The Council is also shown to own sporting rights which are let to R. W. Boden. A caravan appears in the list also, but what kind of caravan, or for what purpose, is not specified.

VALUATION LIST 1920

No.	Name of Occupier.	Name of Owner.	Description of Property.
24	Partington Mrs.	Duke of Westminster	House, land + buildings
25	Fearnall Thos.	"	Land
26	Jones + others	"	"
27	Duke of Westminster	"	Plantations
28	Nickson W.	Cheshire C.C.	House, land + bldgs.
29	Machin	Knowles E.S.	Land.
30	Shallcross Alfred Thos.	Willis Alfred	"
31	Morgan J.	Cheshire C.C.	"
32	Grace Geo.		"
33	Fearnall Hy.	Fearnall Hy	"
34	Shallcross J.P.	J. Cooper	
35	Cooper J	"	Plantations + Pond
36	"	Mrs Burrow	Land
37	"	various	Sporting rights
38	P.O. Telephones	Selves	Tel. Wires.

Approved by the ASSESSMENT COMMITTEE of the TARVIN UNION this 2nd day of Octr. 1920

Many stresses and strains arose from the growth of population, the rise of modern industry and the appearance of the great urban conglomerations. Landowners found their pre-eminence challenged by new industrial wealth and urban aspirations. The gradual deterioration in the status of land led ultimately to the selling-up of estates. In the few short years between 1910 and 1921, great accumulations of land were sold. The landowner's way of life had been made possible by cheap labour. Those in agriculture now had to adjust to a different economic climate.

In 1919 the Huntington Estate, which stretched from the side of the River Dee, through Boughton Heath and as far as Christleton, was offered for auction by the beneficiaries under the will of George Cooper.[115] It will be observed on the map to the below, apart from Mr. Hincks' Butter Bache land and one other, the whole area of Huntington was put on the market. It was divided into twenty-six lots comprising more than thirteen hundred acres.

1919 SALE PLAN – HUNTINGTON ESTATE

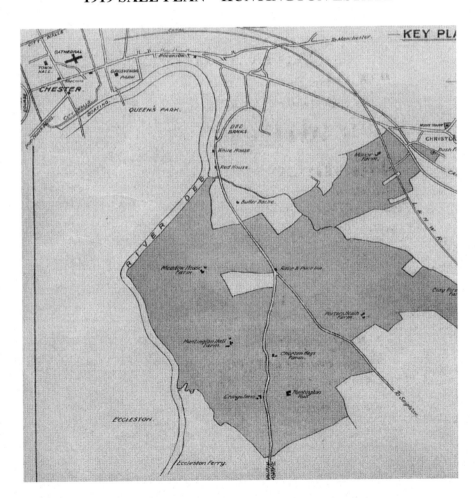

---

[115] Appendix 2.

Seven farms were offered individually which was an outstanding opportunity for farmers to become owners of their own farmland. How many tenants were able to avail themselves of this chance cannot be ascertained. Apart from Huntington Hall, the only other property without a tenant was that of the Grange Farm. The present owner and farmer, Mr. Fred Robinson, supplied the information that his father was successful in his bid for The Grange at the aforesaid auction.

The division and sale of this estate, although due to George Cooper's death, signalled the end of the old landowning way of life in Huntington. It was very much a sign of the times. The Huntington properties sold at this time, however, are still in agricultural use and appearance, apart from the now empty Saighton Army camp, (now being built on).

The pattern of buying and selling continued on a smaller scale. At the time of the sale Huntington Hall was offered as 'a delightful freehold country residence and farm' with over one hundred and twenty-eight acres of 'sound Cheshire dairying land', (schedule, below) together with the Manors and Lordships (or reputed Manors and Lordships) of Huntington and Cheaveley.

THE FIRST SCHEDULE before referred to		
Number on Ordnance Plan 1911 Edition	**Description**	**Quantity**
35	Field	2.195
37	do	3.260
38	do	3.881
39	do	10.417
40	Plantation	.670
41	Field	6.255
42	do	7.032
43	do	15.746
44	do	3.539
45	do	12.443
116	do	13.225
116a	Two Cottages and Gardens	.232
117}	Residence, Lake, Grounds and Homestead	2.684
117a}	do	.017
117b}	do	.250
118	Field	2.264
119	do	7.181
120	do	7.970
120a}	Plantation and Pond	.412
121}	do	.348
265	Field	13.478
266	do	15.065
	Acres	128.564

The plan of 1911 (below) shows the Huntington Hall property holding as a much reduced block of land, no longer stretching from the River Dee but from Aldford Road across to Saighton Lane only.

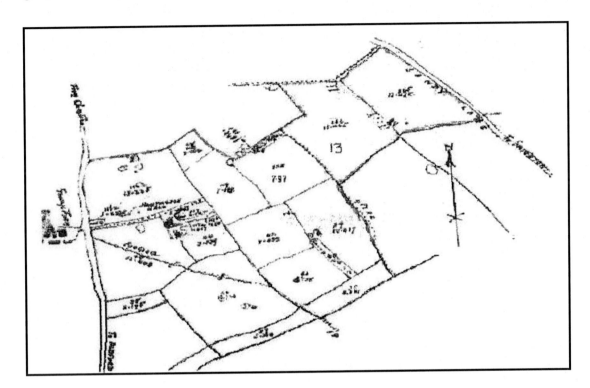

When compared with the key plan of the 1919 sale, it will be easily noted just how considerably the original estate had been reduced. Inspection of a further plan (see below), which was included with the indenture of sale of 4th. August, 1926, shows that four fields had been disposed of, thus reducing the holding by approximately two-fifths.

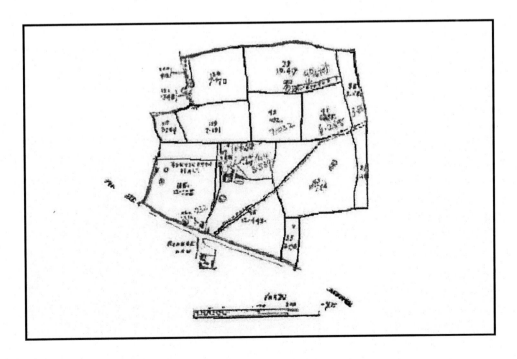

The Sale of Huntington Hall Cottages

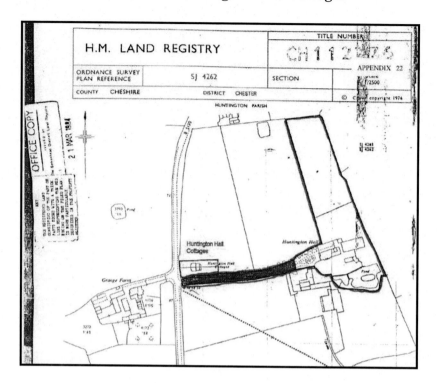

The 'selling-off' of various pieces of land and property from the Huntington Hall holding continued. Two cottages at the side of the entrance were disposed of, followed later by the sale of the stables and a portion of land to the side of the main drive, marked in red on the plan (below) in 1975. The stables, or loose boxes, were eventually completely refurbished and became known as the Stable House.

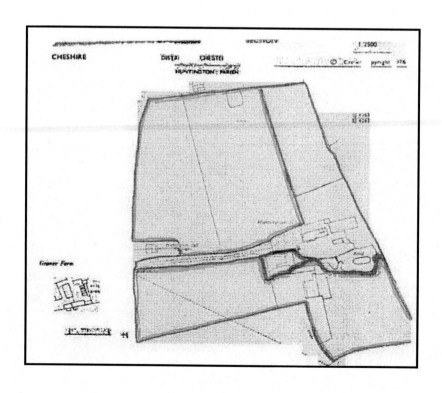

A further sale, a little later, of the area marked in both blue and green on this same plan including an large building, which had probably been a coach house, led to an eventual purchase by a member of a local farming family and the property emerged as Huntington Hall Farm, thus bringing this farm name into use once more. The eventual holding of Huntington Hall is depicted in red on the Land Registry plan of 1976. (Below)

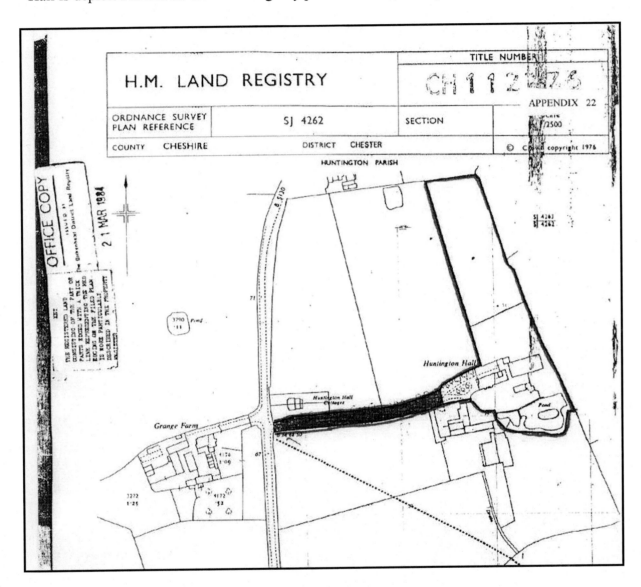

An analysis of these changes, with reference to the plans, underlines the 'whittling down' of property holdings such as Huntington Hall, even after their partition from the original estate, into smaller multiple ownership and, in other cases, modern estate development, which has become so typical a feature of life and the landscape.

The First World War brought all house building to a halt. At the same time changes in social and economic standards, including younger marriage, smaller families, higher wages and more flexible forms of public and private transport, had been gathering momentum in Britain since the end of the nineteenth century. The result of all these changes was a large backlog of demand for houses, each with its own garden. The relatively large amounts of land necessary for this were only available on the outskirts of towns, in places such as Huntington. These private developments enabled many better-class families to move out of congested urban areas to live in semi-rural surroundings. Huntington proved ideal for a number of people.

In the immediate need to overcome the housing shortage resulting from the war, together with a growing social conscience, the Housing and Planning Act of 1919 introduced the principle of state subsidies to help local authorities build houses; thus municipal estates grew alongside the private suburbs on the periphery of towns. As pressures encouraging urban expansion increased, some attempts were made to cope with them. The Town and Country Planning Act of 1932 extended the scope of previous legislation to make almost all classes of land subject to planning control.[116] However, even this measure proved inadequate. Under the 1932 Act it took approximately three years to gain final approval for a scheme. Then, since parliament had to ratify each plan, before any alterations or adjustments could be made, the whole process had to be repeated. It was at this time that housing development began in Huntington.

Butterbache farmhouse is at the Chester end of Huntington, near to the Red House, a public house, on the banks of the Dee, and a short distance from a launching area for boats.

---

[116] J.H. Johnson, Editor, *Suburban Growth,* (London, 1974) p. 54

It was on the Butterbache farm lands that Huntington's housing development started. This is the land, the subject of concern during the Turnpike era that J. C. Hincks envisaged as a prime building position.

It was on the Butterbache Farm lands that the ribbon development of Huntington's housing started. Parcels of land were sold in the 1930s and building commenced. It was in the black and white premises, facing the village green, that Jones and Son, of Love Street, Chester, established a greengrocery business which they continued until fairly recent years.

Huntington Post Office, now extended to incorporate an antiques business, on the opposite side of the road, was also planned as a business premises cum dwelling.

This development continued in both directions along the side of the road. Later this was followed by more housing in the Butterbache Road area behind the village green shops. A study of Ordnance Survey maps of 1954, 1968[117] and 1982,[118] which are pre-A55 dual carriageway, reveal no further change in this building development. As the 1982 map is in colour it is easier to see the relation of places to the River Dee.

Some years were to elapse before the extensive building development of the last twenty years or so when the new estate gradually spread from the land behind Butterbache farmhouse and the Post Office side of Chester Road, Huntington, until it covered the intervening acres and reached Boughton where it joined forces with a new shopping area distinguished by a Sainsbury's store.

Twentieth century church developments

The eventual building development in Huntington led inevitably to an increase in its population which must have put considerable strain on the capacity of Bruera Church. It was on 23rd. September 1938 that the Bachefield Building Company Limited donated land on the westerly side of Huntington Road for Huntington Mission Room.[119] The new Mission Room was opened on Saturday afternoon, 12th. November 1938. Mr. S. Grimshaw "opened" the Room, prior to the Opening Service of Dedication. The Lord Bishop of Chester dedicated the building and preached to a crowded congregation.[120] This Galilee Mission Hall was a little wooden building on the site of the present church, on the Chester Road in Huntington.

HUNTINGTON MISSION HALL

---

[117] Cheshire Record Office, *Map refs. SJ 46 SW 1954 and 1968, 6 inch*
[118] O. S. map, Chester (East) Sheet SJ 46/56, 1:25000, 1982
[119] Cheshire Record Office, P24 / 3193 / 15
[120] Ibid, P24 / 3193 / 14 / 1

The cleric from St. Paul's, Boughton, who was responsible for conducting the services, brought a portable harmonium with him to accompany the hymns. He has descended in local legend as a man of energetic and unusual character who, on arriving, forthrightly charged the absentee parishioners to attend the church services with the vigorous exhortation, "All you heathens, come out".

There were further changes in Huntington's church arrangements due to an alteration of the areas of the parishes of Bruera, Christleton and St. Paul, Chester, when part of the parish of Christleton was transferred to the parish of St. Paul, Chester; part of the parish of St. Paul, Chester, was transferred to the parish of Christleton; and part of the parish of Bruera (the part that was Huntington) was transferred to the parish of St. Paul, Chester.[121]

For a period church services were held in the school which was 'dedicated' for this purpose 17th. November 1985. Finally, however, Huntington got its own church of St. Luke, dedicated and opened by the Bishop of Chester, 5th September 1989. The Chester Chronicle, Friday, September 8, 1989, reported it, somewhat aptly, under the heading 'Godly relief at church opening' and pictured the Bishop and Rural Dean of Chester with the Vicar of St. Luke's.[122]

---

[121] Cheshire Record Office, P24 / 3193 / 9
[122] Chester Library, MF Chester Chronicle, September 8, 1989

St. Luke's is not a consecrated Parish Church but a Parish Centre of Worship. It does not have the legal status of a Parish Church because it was not Diocesan policy at that time. In practical terms this means that anyone wishing to marry at either Christleton or Bruera can do so without the six months' notice usual for non-parishioners.

School development

Building development at Huntington in the 1930s must have inevitably led to an increase in children of school age which must also have put great strain on the Saighton School and its limited resources. On 30th August 1943 Huntington Temporary Council Infants School opened in the Mission Room[123] with Mrs. Helen Jennings as Headmistress.[124] By 1944 the Education Authority decided to increase the school numbers and an assistant teacher was engaged to assist the new Headmistress, Miss M. J. Williams. The problem of broken fencing and thus the welfare of the children was discussed by the Mission Room Committee and the suggestion that the County Council might be approached for some timber, or a permit to obtain some, is a reminder that this was wartime and everything was in very short supply, requiring priority permission.

The school went from strength to strength with numbers rising from 24 pupils in 1944 to 70 or more in 1954, in spite of labouring under extremely sparse and difficult conditions. A report from the Ministry of education on an inspection of 31st May 1948 said,[125] "This Infants' School was opened in these temporary premises (a Mission church) in August 1943. There is one large room 43' x 19'. The local Education Authority provided a small room for storage and offices, including two WCs and urinal (which lead directly from the small vestibule room), and a small area of playground with a hard surface. The rooms are satisfactorily heated by gas radiators but in both rooms the ventilation is inadequate. There are 47 children on roll from 4 years to 7+ years. At 7+ they are transferred and they go either to Aldford C.E. Primary School or to Chester Cherry Grove Council. The local Education Authority provides transport".

---

[123] Appendix 1
[124] Cheshire Record Office, Minute Book of the Managers, SL 60 / 1
[125] Ibid, Log Book, SL 60 / 2

The Report approved highly of the headmistress and the way the school had developed steadily on modern lines under her direction. Indeed it appears to have been a most progressive approach to education especially for that time. There was liberal provision for the children to develop independently and special consideration given to social training. What is particularly interesting is the wholehearted co-operation of the parents, at a time of a more rigid educational system, for what could be described as an experiment in modern methods. They were obviously pleased with their children's progress and happiness at school, thus were appreciative of the success, in spite of the difficulties of inadequate accommodation and resources. They were also probably aware of the various visits from teachers far and wide, including three Nigerian Administrators, who came to study their methods.

The Managers drew the Education Committee's attention to the growing need for suitable premises for primary children and also expressed the hope that steps would be taken at the earliest opportunity to provide a secondary modern school in the Chester Rural area.

'In view of the need for economy', the Director of Education, 30 March 1954, asked the School Managers to defer their request for the provision of a sandpit 'until more favourable circumstances appertain'. They also informed the Managers that the moveable parts for a partition would be provided in the forthcoming financial year and that the proposed Christleton Mixed Secondary Modern School would serve the Huntington area.

The school closed for the Christmas holidays on 20th. December 1957 and the new school in Butterbache Road, Huntington, opened on 6th January 1958. However it was not until Saturday, January 18th. 1958 that the Chester Chronicle carried an article in the District News section on page 4. (Chester's first woman Mayor and the Northern Missionary Congress at Chester, plus the presence of Dr. Temple, Archbishop of York, had proved to be greater highlights). It was reported to be 'a well-planned, light and airy building, consisting of three main classrooms for juniors and two rooms for infants, a spacious hall and a staff room which serves the double duty of a first aid room'. After fifteen years of coping with the extremely limited and difficult conditions and accommodation of the Mission Room, it was agreed to be 'a little palace'.

Like the road through Huntington, the view of the school from the road is undistinguished but when one goes round to the back, beyond the well-surfaced playground, and sees the enclosed 'garden' area where the youngest children play, there is much of the village school atmosphere. The contrast is striking when considering the convenience of a school set in the housing area today and the difficulties of access, weather and distance in those early years.

HUNTINGTON SCHOOL FRONT AND PLAY AREA AT THE REAR

Nowadays when the children leave Huntington Community Primary School for further education they have the choice of the Bishop's Blue Coat Church of England High School, Vaughan's Lane, Boughton, known familiarly as Bishop's High, or Christleton High School. There are also the noted King's School for boys and the Queen's School for girls in Chester for those who may wish to seek entrance.

The dichotomy of present day Huntington

Pevsner did not think there was any building of note in Huntington and Cheaveley. Saighton Grange is the only one in this area to be discussed in the Cheshire section of 'The Buildings of England'. As he says 'except for a few houses like Saighton Grange, inhabited by men of wealth and influence (in this case an Abbot), stone was never used extensively in Cheshire for domestic purposes. Even until the early part of the seventeenth century, the large majority of this county's houses, as well as a fair sprinkling of village churches, were half-timbered, for oaks grew here in profusion until the extravagant felling under Elizabeth I'.[126]

There is nothing left of the early Huntington Hall, the dwelling place of Sir George Beverley, which William Webb described in the early part of the seventeenth century, saying 'the capital manor is a very neat house of timber'.[127] The site is now home to Old Hall Country Club advertised as 'the perfect place to either unwind or simply relax and unwind', in a tranquil rural setting.

Even so, there are older buildings in the 'rural half' of Huntington which have been designated of architectural interest. The Grange farmhouse, Grade II, of three storeys, on the west side of the Aldford Road, Map reference SJ 46 SW, situated opposite the drive to Huntington Hall, is dated 1653.

---

[126] N. Pevsner & N. Hubbard, *The Buildings of England, Cheshire,* (Middlesex, 1978), p.46
[127] Cheshire Sheaf Number 39

Its upper storey was rebuilt in the late eighteenth century and has a late nineteenth century addition to the rear. It is of English garden wall bond and Flemish bond brick, rectangular in plan, with a Welsh slate roof and two brick chimneys.

HUNTINGTON HALL

The present Huntington Hall, Map reference SJ 46 SW, once known as Little Huntington Hall, is no longer counted of special architectural interest now that Grade III has been abolished. In Chester Rural District Council's report circa 1980 it was described as a seventeenth century, much altered and modernised house and farm buildings. The house is of two storeys and roughcast, with a slate roof of two parallel ridges.

The interior has been much altered, including the windows. There is a modern staircase. It may contain the shell of an early house, including the roof timbers. The cellar is old and interesting. The deeds are from 1670 but a twelfth century house is believed to have been on the site.

The exterior of Huntington Hall today is very much as it is pictured in the sale brochure of the Huntington Estate in 1919[128] but the roof had to be completely replaced in 1977 due to death watch beetle in the timbers, thus they are no longer original. There appeared to be little change in the interior, apart from decoration, in 1984, with the exception of two extra bathrooms and the loss of one of the bedrooms. The cellar is certainly old and interesting. It is entered through a trapdoor in the back passage leading to the kitchen quarters. The lower part of its walls are of sandstone and there is a brick wall at one end, giving the impression that it was built as a screen. Beyond the paved yard is a deep well, beautifully and meticulously lined with bricks. During the complete overhaul and refurbishing of the 1970s, it was discovered that the rear end of the house had been an addition. The design of the building suggests an earlier central portion with later additions.

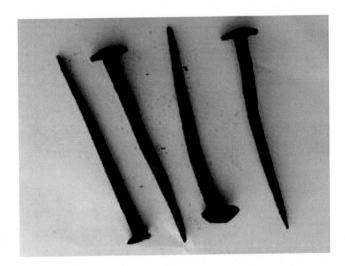

Handmade nails from the original roof

Cheaveley Hall farmhouse, Map reference SJ 46 SW, farther along and on the west side of the Aldford Road, is a late seventeenth century building with eighteenth and nineteenth century alterations and additions

---

[128] Appendix 2

Meadowhouse farmhouse (shown below), in Meadow Lane, Map reference SJ 46 SW, is a Grade II, early eighteenth century, T-shaped building, with twentieth century additions, of English bond orange brick. The roof is of Welsh slate and has a central ridge brick chimney. There is an early eighteenth century, Grade II barn thirty metres west, an L-shaped range of outbuildings with later eighteenth and later twentieth century additions.

Walker's flower nursery is on land near to the fork in the road, not far from the Rake and Pikel, and opposite the site of the deserted Saighton Army Camp, which has been under discussion for development. Close by is the Chester southerly by-pass, part of the infrastructure of our modern road system, which can be looked down on from the modern road bridge, and marks a dividing line between the farmland area of Huntington and its developed part.

North West Water's water treatment works also acts as a division of the land in the developed area in Huntington from its farming sector. It is the biggest abstractor of water from the Dee. This works is the Company's largest and is among the top three water treatment works in the country. It is also one of the largest water treatment works in Europe, though probably few local people are aware of its extent and importance. The large and complex plant consists of four separate water treatment streams and has the capacity to supply up to 400 million litres of quality drinking water to the taps of approximately 1.7 million customers in Cheshire and Merseyside.

From Victorian days Liverpool had taken most of its water from Lake Vyrnwy in North Wales and from the reservoirs at Rivington near Bolton. By 1959 these sources were no longer sufficient for the needs of the city and the surrounding districts. In that year work began at the new plant at Huntington in Chester. This work ran in conjunction with the development of the Dee Regulation Scheme. Commissioned in 1963 it initially supplied 146 megalitres (32 million gallons) daily; since then two further phases have been added and brought it to the present daily capacity of 91 million gallons.

Huntington Village Hall (shown below) is tucked away in the Butterbache Road area. It is approached via a path which runs between two houses and is small and unassuming. It is the centre of village activities. Like the school, it projects a feeling and an image of a small and close-knit village community.

Nowadays the village shops number a general store, a newsagents, a hairdressing establishment, a chip shop, and a dentist, as well as the Post Office cum Huntington Antiques. Some yards up from the village centre, at the corner of Chester Road and Gorse Way, the new road leading down to Sainsbury's Boughton development, is a large motor car sales garage, dealing in new Honda cars as well as a range of used vehicles, a far cry from the pony and trap days in the early nineteen hundreds.

The contrast between the two 'different parts' of Huntington can be appreciated on the aerial photograph shown on the next two pages. It can be seen how the modern dual carriageway of the southerly by-pass and the Water Works effectively divide the rural and 'ancient' from the urban and modern.

Chester is regarded as one of Britain's most important historic cities and is probably best known for its wealth of historic buildings within the city walls, its Roman remains, the Rows, the River Dee and the Groves. An important aspect of the character of the City is the open areas and woodland which, in places, form green 'wedges' separating the old part of the city from its suburbs. These areas provide a landscape setting for the City and secure a relationship between the built environment and the open countryside.

The Caldy Valley at Huntington is considered to be important in this respect, forming an area of parkland between two large areas of new housing. It is also a small wetland area and as Cheshire has few areas of wetlands this is an important possession as well as an attractive amenity. It has remained unspoilt. A pair of swans and various ducks swim on a large pond and it is a regular venue for owners to exercise their dogs and small children to venture on bicycles wearing their colourful safety helmets.

2685 0

J.A.STORY AND PARTNERS
92-94 CHURCH ROAD
MITCHAM SURREY.

CONTACT SCALE

1:10,000

DATE

30/5/85

COPYRIG
CHESHIR
COUNCIL

85

J.A.STORY AND PARTNERS
92-94 CHURCH ROAD
MITCHAM SURREY

CONTACT SCALE

1:10,000

DATE

30/5/85

COPYRIGH
CHESHIRE
COUNCIL

2685 0

CONCLUSION

This research into Huntington's roots has revealed how much has rested on land, on the possession of land, in the getting of it, in the development of it, and the management of it, from Sir Richard Cotton, the arch Tudor 'on the make', to Sir George Beverley, the 'first gentleman' and founder of the first resident family, to succeeding estate owners, and on through the years of the most important economic, social and technological changes that influenced the pattern of rural England in the nineteenth century.

It has shown how the vicissitudes and resultant changes consequent on far-reaching causes of national and international affairs on the land-owning hierarchy in the nineteenth century contributed to the gradual deterioration in the status of land and the pre-eminence of the old land-owning hierarchy whose way of life had been made possible by cheap labour.

A further twist and turn of fate in the fortunes of many of the old landowners can be followed in the solving of drainage problems on the heavy clay soils of the area through the invention of the circular tile. It is evident that the enthusiasm for high, or intensive, farming together with the introduction of chemical fertilizers and farm machinery, which then led to a demand for a commensurate improvement in farm building, and which required heavy investment by the landowner, was a burden of exceptional weight which, although it could not be foreseen, had come at a time when inevitable and inexorable changes would press heavily. It was a time when only those landowners with other means of income, such as the Grosvenors, could adjust to the new commercial approach to farming.

Improved communication and the breaking down of rural isolation through the coming of the turnpike roads played their part in slowly transforming rural Huntington. The growth of industrialisation and the opening up of rapidly growing urban markets in adjacent areas such as Merseyside, together with the introduction of compulsory schooling, the effect of union activity in the country at large and the extension of the franchise, were all influential in gradually drawing the rural worker into the current of contemporary life.

The change of outlook among the labouring population in the countryside added further to the stresses caused by the challenge of industrial change and led to a gradual deterioration in the status of land and of the landowner. It was this that led ultimately to the selling-up of estate land.

It is in the differences of landownership, that the answer lies as to why there was development in Huntington and not in Saighton and Bruera. The Grosvenor Estate consolidated their land holding and as a result have kept control. It was the eventual development of the Butterbache land fronting the turnpike road, as Mr Hincks had envisaged, that was but a short distance to Spital Boughton, and thus to Chester, that led to the growth of Huntington as a 'roadside' township. This development has been contained by the predominance of the surrounding farmland.

The 'influence' of Chester with its loss of commercial importance due to the silting up of the Dee also needs some consideration. Had the navigation of the river been solved could Chester have then expanded into a modern day port with all that would entail? What effect might this have had on the surrounding areas of the city, such as Huntington? Or would the value of its good farmland have kept its rural importance? It has to be remembered that industrial development requires a sufficient area of land at an economical, if not cheap, price. It is possible that land in this area of study would not have met these requirements. Then the proximity of the Grosvenor Estate would, of a certainty, have brought forth strong representations from that quarter. Once more landowning is a factor.

This search has uncovered and illustrated how the history of the land and its owners is linked inextricably with the history and development of Huntington. It can be seen how and why the dichotomy of this village arose.

APPENDIX 1

Street plan showing position of Huntington Mission Hall

Cheshire Record Office, P24 / 3193 / 15

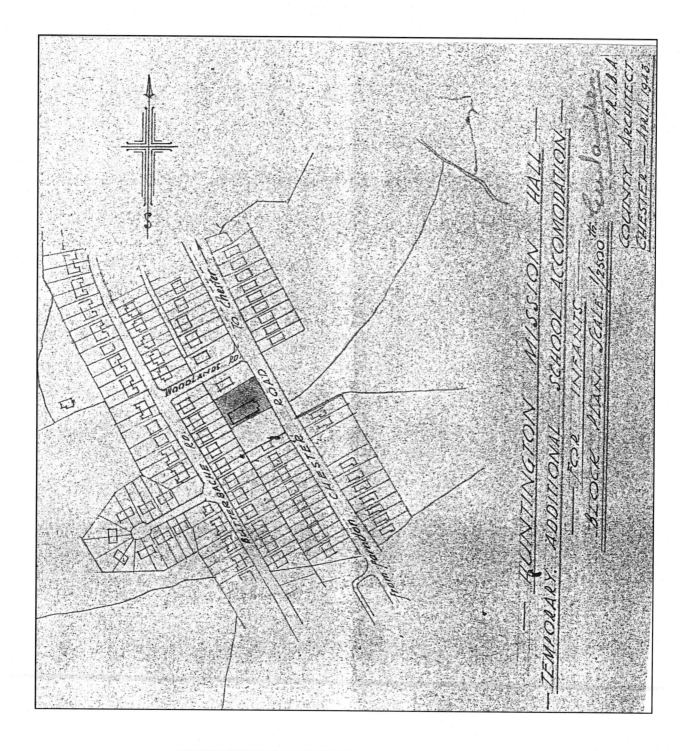

**HUNTINGTON MISSION HALL TEMPORARY
ADDITIONAL SCHOOL ACCOMODATION**

APPENDIX 2

A selection of properties from the 1919 sale brochure of the Huntington Estate

CHESHIRE.

In the Townships of Huntington, Christleton, Rowton, Saighton
and Great Boughton,
and close to the Historic City of Chester.

—·—·—·—·—·—·—·—

Particulars

With Views, Plans and Conditions of Sale

OF THE

VALUABLE FREEHOLD

Agricultural Estate

KNOWN AS THE

"Huntington" Estate,

Comprising the Manors or Lordships of Huntington, Cheaveley and Christleton :

Charming Country Reside⸺⸺ ⸺ known as "Huntington Hall,"

Huntington Hall Farm,	Clay Pits Farm,
Grange Farm,	"Rake and Pikel" Public House,
Churton Heyes Farm,	Manor Farm,
Meadow House Farm,	Manor House,
Porter's Heath Farm,	Cottages and Gardens,
	Building & Accommodation Lands,

THE WHOLE EXTENDING TO OVER

1,342 Acres,

Which will be OFFERED FOR AUCTION, by

MESSRS.

FRANK LLOYD & SONS,

At the GROSVENOR HOTEL, CHESTER,

On Saturday, the 24th day of May, 1919,

At 2 o'clock,

Either together or in the following or such other Lots as may be decided upon at the time of Sale.

Solicitors :
MESSRS. BARKER & ROGERSON,
12, White Friars,
CHESTER.

Auctioneers Offices :
St. Oswald's Chambers, St. Werburgh St.,
CHESTER ;
Head Office: WREXHAM ;
Also at Whitchurch and Crewe

HUNTINGTON HALL
From the North

HUNTINGTON HALL, RUSTIC BRIDGE AND LAKE
From the South

**THE ENTRANCE TO HUNTINGTON HALL
AND COTTAGES**

HUNTINGTON HALL FARM

FARM YARD AND BUILDINGS

THE GRANGE FARM
Nearly opposite the Entrance to Huntington Hall on the
Chester and Farndon Main Road

THE MEADOW FARM

"RAKE AND PIKEL INN"
At the junction of the Saighton, the Farndon and the Chester Roads

APPENDIX 3

Turnpike Road Plan – Huntington portion

Cheshire Record Office, QRP69 / 1

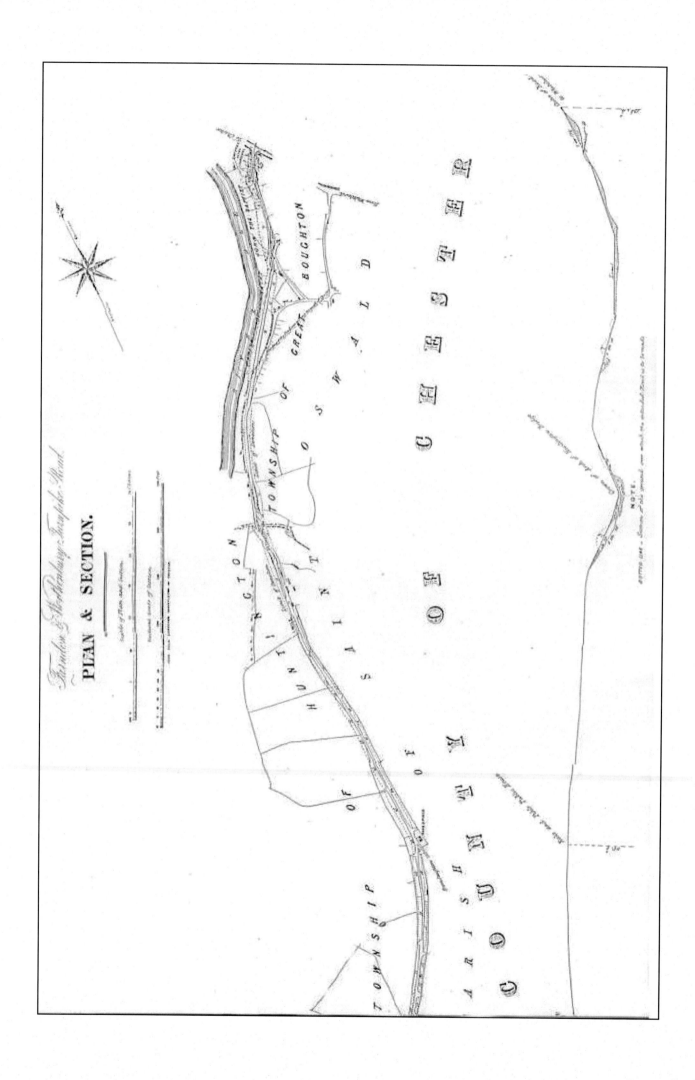

London & Northampton Turnpike Road

PLAN & SECTION.

Scale of Plan and Section.

Vertical Scale of Section.

TOWNSHIP OF HUNTINGTON

TOWNSHIP OF GREAT OSWALD

BOUGHTON

COUNTY OF HUNTINGDON

CHESTER

TOWNSHIP OF

NOTE.

APPENDIX 4

New School Specifications

and

Archaeology Survey

The village school (Bruera) was built around 1830 by voluntary subscription. It consisted of a small brick building to house up to 70 children. It continued in use until replaced by the Saighton school. The continued demolition of houses around the village and relocation of the population in Saighton one mile distant made this move inevitable.

P 24 / 4

SCHOOL BUILDING SPECIFICATION 1863

Specification of Works to be done in the erection of a school for the Most Noble the Marquis of Westminster on a sight at Saighton in the County of Chester in Accordance with the Plans and Drawings prepared for that purpose.

Conditions :　　The Contractor or Contractors will be required to execute all the work enumerated in the specification to the entire satisfaction of the Architect or who he may appoint to act for him　　And in conformity with the plans and Drawings prepared for the purpose, find all kinds of materials save such as are hereinafter mentioned. Provide all tool-utensils, jacks and scaffolding and everything necefsary to complete The Works in a satisfactory and workmanlike manner - pay compensation for or make good any damage that may be done by the workmen or Contractors to adjoining property, or land in the execution of the contract or contracts

p. 2　　The works as hereinafter specified must be completed as well as any additions or alterations in the said works in a good and substantial manner and in case any such alterations or additions are required during the progrefs of the works, the contractor must follow the written directions of the architect exprefsing the nature of such alterations, additions or deviations, and the expence hereof must be added or deducted from the amount of contract. As the case may be the value of the same being fixed by the Architect or who he may appoint and should any damage or injury happen to the works from the Act of God or the wilfullnefs of man, or from bad or defective workmanship or materials or any other cause, such injury or defects shall be made good at the expence of the Contractor or Contractors, whom it may specially concern　---

p. 3　　The whole of the works to be completed next coming ------ or a forfeit of ----- Pounds for every week the works remain unfinished afterwards payments to be made in ------ instalments on the certificate of the Architect. The last one being paid in a reasonable time after the buildings are completed and all refuse materials and rubbish carted away and the buildings left clean and perfect.

p. 4　　Excavate. To dig out the Ground to sound bottom (or rock) to required depth -------- also ---------- the soil and rock beneath the floors that are to be wood. Dig out also for the Ashpit and privies And Tile floors ------ Dig out the yard and level around the building -------------------- Rubbish must also be removed as it accumulates during the progrefs of the Works

p. 5   The Contractor is to pull down the Cottages on or near the site - drefs all the sound brick and stones for re-use in the foundations and lay aside neatly piled all refuse materials which are not to be used and which are to remain the property of the Noble Proprietor

      Bricklayer.   To build all the walls in brickwork in old English bond of the respective thicknefses with good mortar well flushed or grouted, in the proportions of one best Welsh lime to two of sharp and clean sand. The Bricks are to be supplied to the Contractor and laid down on the site at 16 / - per thousand from Plats rough

      The school clafs room, Entrance and laundry to be wholly lined with the best Staffordshire white Bricks equal to sample, and to be had of Mr. Oakden of Princefs Street Manchester   ....

p. 6   properly build and form all the smoke flues, well *harfing* the same with Common Mortar and Cow dung mixed And form fresh air flues with grids built in at the back of each fireplace on the outside ---- Coat all the foundations with asphalt ½ in. thick

p. 7   Provide and set in the work all air and vermin grids - and grids for drainage of Privies - and the Building as shown on the plan as directed

      Mason :

p. 9   Slater and Plasterer

p. 10   Plumber Glazier and Painter

p. 12   Carpenter and Joiner

p. 15   Cupola   ....

      All the Carting to be done by the Tenantry

Moat in Huntington Parish

Susan Reynolds and Wayne Cocroft reported that students from Chester College surveyed two moats to the south of Chester during a short archaeological survey course.

The first of these moats, shown below, scheduled ancient monument 123, Cheshire SMR 1945, is located at SJ 4295 6200, 23m above O. D. in a locally dominating position on the crest of the western escarpment of the River Dee over glacial till deposits. The moat straddles Beggars Brook which forms the parish boundary between Huntington and Saighton parishes, both parishes are within Broxton Hundred. The place name Huntington, meaning 'hunting hill, place where the hunting was done' (Dodgson 1972, 117), at Domesday was held as the manor of Huntington and Cheavely by St. Werburgh's church in Chester (VCH 1987, 344). The moat is one of three within Huntington parish, the largest at Huntington Hall, 800m to the north, has been identified as 'the grange of the abbot of Chester at Huntington' referred to in 1348 (Dodgson 1972, 117). The third of these moats (Cheshire SMR 1946) lies within mixed woodland about 2km to the north.[129]

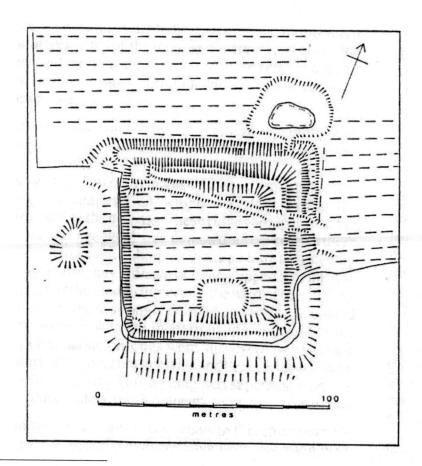

[129] Medieval Settlement Research Group Annual Report 6 1991

APPENDIX 5

Huntington Life

Rose Queens

Children of Huntington

Friends at Play 1959

**Fancy Dress Parade Competition
1956 Mission Room Huntington**

View across the fields and Caldy Valley

**Victory Party St. George's
Mission Hall 1945**

Christmas Party in the Mission Room 1943 - 1945

Café at Reg Lowe's Dance Hall

APPENDIX 6

Huntington Census 1841 – 1891

| Place | HOUSES | | NAMES | Age and Sex | | PROFESSION, TRADE, EMPLOYMENT, or of INDEPENDENT MEANS | WHERE BORN | |
	Uninhabited or Building	Inhabited	of each Person who abode therein the preceding Night	Male	Female		Whether born in name County	Whether born in Scotland, Ireland or Foreign Parts
Huntington		/	Joseph Parker	60		Farmer	Y	
			Elizabeth Parker		34		Y	
			William Parker	30			Y	
			Mary Ann Parker		25		Y	
			Katherine Swindly		15	Female Servant	Y	
			Thomas Jones	14		Male Servant	Y	
			James Hughson	14			Y	
			Elizabeth Bennet		20	Female Servant	Y	
		/	Richard Phoenix	70		Publican	N	
			Ann Phoenix		70		Y	
			William Phoenix	29		Farmer	Y	
			Martha Phoenix		29		Y	
			William Phoenix	5			Y	
			Richard Phoenix	2			Y	
			Samuel Houghfield	6			Y	
		/	James Hughson	34		Agricultural labourer	Y	
			Jane Hughson		35		Y	
			Ann Hughson		60		Y	
			Thomas Hughson	35			Y	
			Sarah Hughson		22		Y	
			William Hughson	19		Agricultural labourer	Y	
			Elizabeth Hughson		18		Y	
		/	Thomas Anson	74		Agricultural labourer	Y	
			Jane Anson		70		Y	
		/	Robert Salmon	30		Farmer	y	
			Hannah Salmon		30		y	
			Mary Ann Salmon		3		y	
			Joseph Salmon	2			y	
			Thomas Salmon	1			y	
			William Young	20		Male Servant	y	
			William Howde	15		Male Servant	y	
			George Huse	15		Male Servant	y	
			Hannah White		20	Female Servant	y	
			Ann Malt		25	Female Servant	y	
			Ann Dutton		13		y	
		/	Letitiece Thomas		73		y	
			Samuel Thomas	30		Agricultural labourer	y	
			Ann Thomas		6		y	
		/	Charles Taylor	30		Agricultural labourer	y	
			Mary Taylor		28		y	
			Ann Taylor		8		y	
			Samuel Taylor	5			y	
			Thomas Taylor	2			y	
			Martha Taylor		1		y	
		/	James Harnott	54		Agricultural labourer	y	
			Mary Harnott		66		y	
			Mary Price		28		y	
			Frances Price		1		y	
		/	Elizabeth Lockley		80		Y	
			Elizabeth Lockley		30		Y	
			Ann Lockley		6		y	
			George Lockley	3			y	
			Edward lockley		5 Months		y	
			Sharlotte Davies		7 Months		y	
			Margaret Littler		23	Female Servant	Y	
		/	John Hughson	28		Agricultural labourer	y	
			Elizabeth Hughson		28		y	
			Mary Hughson		9		y	
			Jane Hughson		7		y	

Place	HOUSES		NAMES	Age and Sex		PROFESSION, TRADE, EMPLOYMENT, or of INDEPENDENT MEANS	WHERE BORN	
	Uninhabited or Building	Inhabited	of each Person who abode therein the preceding Night	Male	Female		Whether born in name County	Whether born in Scotland, Ireland or Foreign Parts
			William Hughson	5			Y	
			John Hughson	2			Y	
		/	Thomas Parker	25		Farmer	y	
			Thomas Gerrard	24		Male Servant	y	
			William Littler	20		Male Servant	y	
			Thomas Parry	18		Male Servant	y	
			Edward Fletcher	17		Male Servant	y	
			Edward Formstone	13		Male Servant	y	
			John Hughes	13		Male Servant	y	
			Elizabeth Salisbury		33	Female Servant	y	
			Mary Williams		20	Female Servant	y	
			Elizabeth Allen		20	Female Servant	y	
		/	Thomas Jones	35		Farmer	y	
			Ann Jones		35		Y	
			Mary Williams		14	Female Servant	y	
			John Hulse	20		Male Servant	y	
			Samuel Fleet	18		Male Servant	y	
			Joseph Foster	18		Male Servant	y	
			Thomas Fleet	14			y	
			Elizabeth Pover		30	Female Servant	Y	
			Mary Fleet		17	Female Servant	Y	
		/	John Goulbourn	36		Farmer	Y	
			Ann Goulborn		33		N	
			Mary Goulborn		6		y	
			Ann Goulborn		3		y	
			Elizabeth Goulborn		1		y	
			Jane Goulborn		2 Months		y	
			Emma Goulborn		35	Independent	y	
			John Tilston	60		Independent	y	
			Samuel Edwards	20			y	
			John Morgan	15			y	
			Joseph Taylor	12		Male Servant	y	
			Martha Liversage		20	Male Servant	N	
			Mary Liversage		15	Male Servant	N	
			Rebecca Deane		15		Y	
			Martha Davies		14		Y	
		/	Thomas Davies	42		Agricultural labourer	y	
			Sarah Davies		45		y	
			William Davies	22		Wheelwright	y	
		/	John Littler	38		Millwright	y	
			Mary Littler		36		N	
			Ann Littler		9		y	
			James Littler	7			y	
			Frances Littler		5		y	
			John Littler	2			y	
		/	William Wrench	70		Farmer	y	
			William Wrench	30			y	
			Mary Wrench		35		y	
			Ann Wrench		30		y	
			Elizabeth Wrench		25		y	
			Jane Kemp		70	Independent	y	
			Samuel Morgan	20		Male Servant	y	
			Robert Hughson	15		Male Servant	y	
			Thomas Taylor	15		Male Servant	y	
			Mary Wilson		25	Female Servant	y	
			Jane Formstone		20	Female Servant	y	
			Jane Owens		15	Female Servant	y	
		/	Thomas Parlington	25		Agricultural labourer	Y	
			Ann Parlington		22		y	

| Place | HOUSES | | NAMES | Age and Sex | | PROFESSION, TRADE, EMPLOYMENT, or of INDEPENDENT MEANS | WHERE BORN | |
	Uninhabited or Building	Inhabited	of each Person who abode therein the preceding Night	Male	Female		Whether born in name County	Whether born in Scotland, Ireland or Foreign Parts
			William Parlington	1			y	
		/	John Walker	42		Agricultural labourer	y	
			Ann Walker		36		y	
			James Walker	14			y	
			Sarah Walker		8		y	
			Mary Walker		6		y	
			Hannah Walker		5		y	
			Eliza Walker		2		y	
			Rebecca Walker		3 Months		Y	
		/	George Brassey	32		Game Keeper	y	
			Mary Brassey		30		Y	
			Richard Brassey	9			y	
			Harriett Brassey		7		y	
			Elizabeth Brassey		2		y	
			George Brassey	4 Months			y	
		/	William Hughson	56		Agricultural labourer	Y	
			Elizabeth Hughson		65		Y	
		/	Richard Fryar	60		Farmer	y	
			Ann Fryar		50		y	
			George Fryar	90			y	
			William Fryar	20			y	
			Jane Fryar		15		y	
			Ann Fryar		15		y	
			Richard Fryar	10			y	
			William Bennet	10		Male Servant	Y	

No. of Householder's Schedule	Name of Street, Place or Road and Name or No. of House	Name and Surname of each Person who abode in the house, on the Night of 30th March, 1851	Relation to Head of Family	Condition	Male	Female	Rank, Profession or Occupation	Where born	Whether blind, deaf or dumb
1	Farndon Road	Daniel Lea	Head	Married	34		Farmer of 75 Acres, Labour	Cheshire, Kelsall	
	Farm House	Mary Lea	Wife	Married		28		Cheshire, Overton	
		Richard Lea	Son	Unmarried	4			Cheshire, Ashton	
		John Lea	Son	Unmarried	2			Cheshire, Kelsall	
		Margaret Lea	Daughter	Unmarried		0		Cheshire, Huntington	
		William Borsley	Servant	Unmarried	20		Farm Labourer	Cheshire, Kelsall	
		Samuel Wadson	Servant	Unmarried	16		Farm Labourer	Cheshire, Kelsall	
		Martha Miller	Servant	Unmarried		27	House Servant	Cheshire, Delamere	
		Ellen Peninton	Servant	Unmarried		14	House Servant	Cheshire, Delamere	
2	Farndon Road	William Huson	Head	Married	65		Farmer of 3 Acres	Cheshire, Saighton	
		Catherine Huson	Wife	Married		53		Cheshire, Cristlenton	
3	Meadow House	Thomas Trappes	Head	Married	70		Retired Master Mariner	Yorkshire, Nedd	
		Eliza Trappes	Wife	Married		66		Ireland, Drogerty	
4	Meadow House	John Walker	Head	Married	52		Balif of 140 Acres, 1 Labourer	Cheshire, Wacton	
		Ann Walker	Wife	Married		46		Cheshire, Morpeth	
		Eliza Walker	Daughter	Unmar.		12		Cheshire, Huntington	
		Rebecca Walker	Daughter	Unmar.		10		Cheshire, Huntington	
		Margaret Walker	Daughter	Unmar.		6		Cheshire, Huntington	
		Elizabeth Walker	Daughter	Unmar.		3		Cheshire, Huntington	
5	Boat House	James Harriot	Head	Widower	66		Ferry Man	Cheshire, Leighton	
		Sarah Harriot	Neice	Unmarried		20	Servant	Cheshire, Huxley	
6	Chealey Farm	John Goulburn	Head	Widower	47		Farmer of 200 Acres 4 Labours	Cheshire, Huntington	
		Mary Goulburn	Daughter	Unmarried		16		Cheshire, Huntington	
		Ann Goulburn	Daughter	Unmarried		13		Cheshire, Huntington	
		Elizabeth Goulburn	Daughter	Unmarried		11		Cheshire, Huntington	
		Jane Goulburn	Daughter	Unmarried		10		Cheshire, Huntington	
		Mary Badcock	Servant	Unmarried		28	House Servant	Cheshire, Spurstow	
		Mary Thomas	Servant	Unmarried		22	House Servant	Cheshire, Churton	
		Ann Manley	Servant	Unmarried		14	House Servant	Cheshire, Aldford	
		James Taylor	Servant	Unmarried	19		Farm Labourer	Cheshire, Saighton	
		John Speed	Servant	Unmarried	16		Farm Labourer	Cheshire, Aldford	
		John Taylor	Servant	Unmarried	13		Farm Labourer	Cheshire, Saighton	
7	Chealey Lodge	Thomas Davies	Head	Married	54		Farm Labourer	Cheshire, Malpas	
		Sarah Davies	Wife	Married		60		Cheshire, Tarvin	
		William Davies	Son	Married	32		Master Wheelwright,1 Man, 2 Boys	Cheshire, Handley	
		Ann Davies	Son's Wife	Married		25		Cheshire, Chester	
8	Chealey Lodge	Robert Jones	Head	Married	35		Farm Labourer	Flintshire, Hope	
		Sarah Jones	Wife	Married		33		Flintshire, Kinnerton	
		John Jones	Son	Unmar.	7			Cheshire, Aldford	
9	Farm House	Thomas Jones	Head	Married	47		Farmer of 240 Acres, 3 Labs.	Cheshire, Barton	
	Farndon Road	Sarah Jones	Wife	Married		29		Cheshire, Weaverton	
		Thomas Jones	Son	Unmarried	1			Cheshire, Huntington	
		Mary Nickson	Servant	Unmarried		32	Dairy Maid	Cheshire, Dunham	
		Ann Dodd	Servant	Unmarried		23	House Maid	Cheshire, Tattenhall	
		Jane Bunghell	Servant	Unmarried		14	Nurse Maid	Cheshire, Chester	
		William Newbrook	Servant	Unmarried	19		Farm Labourer	Cheshire, Clotton	
		John Hughes	Servant	Unmarried	20		Farm Labourer	Cheshire, Chester	
		John Hughson	Servant	Unmarried	13		Farm Labourer	Cheshire, Huntington	
10	Farm House	Robert Bover Hinchliffe	Head	Married	41		Solicitor in Practice,farming 150 Acre	Cheshire, Barthomley	
	Farndon Road	Elisabeth Hinchliffe	Wife	Married		37		Lancashire, Warrington	
		Georgina H. E. Hinchliffe	Daughter	Unmarried		9		Cheshire, Poole	
		John Parkes	Carpenter	Married	45		Carpenter	Cheshire, Nantwich	
		Emma Roberts	Servant	Unmarried		27	Dairy maid	Flintshire, Gresford	
		Emma Edwards	Servant	Unmarried		18	Housemaid	Flintshire, Gresford	
		Rebecca Dean	Servant	Unmarried		27	Cook	Cheshire, Tilstone	
		Joseph Poole	Servant	Unmarried	14		Cowboy	Cheshire, Chester	
		John Owen	Servant	Married	45		Farm Servant	Cheshire, Poole	
		Mary Owen	Servant Wife	Married		37	Farm Servant's Wife	Cheshire, Worleston	
		Maria Owen	Servant Daurghter	Unmarried		7	Farm Servant's Daughter	Cheshire, Kenhall	Blind
		Joseph Owen	Visitor	Married	66		Letter Carrier	Cheshire, Worleston	
11	Cottage	Samuel Thomas	Head	Married	40		Agricultural labourer	Cheshire, Huntington	
	Farndon Road	Ann Thomas	Wife	Married		29		Cheshire, Handley	
		Martha Thomas	Daughter	Unmarried		7		Cheshire, Huntington	
		Sarah Thomas	Daughter	Unmarried		4		Cheshire, Huntington	
		Catherine Thomas	Daughter	Unmarried		0		Cheshire, Huntington	
		James Formstone	Lodger	Married	23		Agricultural labourer	Cheshire, Handley	
		Mary Formstone	Lodger	Married		19		Cheshire, Huntington	
	1 House Uninhabited								
12	Cottage	Thomas Huson	Head	Married	41		Agricultural labourer	Cheshire, Huntington	
	Farndon Road	Elisabeth Huson	Wife	Married		42		Cheshire, Huntington	
		Ann Huson	Daughter	Unmarried		15		Cheshire, Huntington	
		George Huson	Son	Unmarried	12			Cheshire, Huntington	
		Edward Huson	Son	Unmarried	10			Cheshire, Huntington	
		Elisabeth Huson	Daughter	Unmarried		6		Cheshire, Huntington	
13	Cottage	John Huson	Head	Married	40		Agricultural labourer	Cheshire, Huntington	
	Farndon Road	Elisabeth Huson	Wife	Married		38		Flintshire, Bangor	

No. of Householder's Schedule	Name of Street, Place or Road and Name or No. of House	Name and Surname of each Person who abode in the house, on the Night of 30th March, 1851	Relation to Head of Family	Condition	Age of Male	Age of Female	Rank, Profession or Occupation	Where born	Whether blind, deaf or dumb
		Jane Huson	Daughter	Unmarried		17		Cheshire, Huntington	
		William Huson	Son	Unmarried	15			Cheshire, Huntington	
		John Huson	Son	Unmarried	12			Cheshire, Huntington	
		Thomas Huson	Son	Unmarried	6			Cheshire, Huntington	
		Robert Huson	Son	Unmarried	3			Cheshire, Huntington	
		James Huson	Son	Unmarried	0			Cheshire, Huntington	
14	Hinks House	Helen Maria Penny	Head	Unmarried		25	Governess	Middlesex, Pentonville	
	Farndon Road	Mary Hincks	Pupil	Unmarried		14	Scholar at home	Yorkshire, Kirby Hiske	
		Elisabeth Esther Hincks	Pupil	Unmarried		13	Scholar at home	Yorkshire, Kirby Hiske	
		Maria Hincks	Pupil	Unmarried		12	Scholar at home	Yorkshire, Kirby Hiske	
		Ann Hall	Servant	Unmarried		21	Lady's Maid	Yorkshire, Kirby Hiske	
		Mary Ann Teesdale	Servant	Unmarried		21	Cook	Durham, Haindrop	
		Thomas Walton	Servant	Unmarried	13		Page	York	
		William Boddy	Head	Married	27		Farmer Bailiff of 140 Acres, 10 Labours	Yorkshire, Kirby Hiske	
		Sarah Boddy	Wife	Married		28	Bailiff's Wife	Yorkshire, Thirsk	
		William Boddy	Son	Unmarried	3			Yorkshire, Sandbuttor	
		Mary Ellen Boddy	Daughter	Unmarried		2		Yorkshire, Thirsk	
		Margaret Boddy	Daughter	Unmarried		0		Yorkshire, Sand Hutton	
		John Holdsworth	Servant	Unmarried	17		Farm Servant	Yorkshire, Lesh	
		Ann Lockley	Servant	Unmarried		15	Nurse	Cheshire, Huntington	
		John Jones	Servant	Widower	69		Farm Labourer	Cheshire, Huntington	
15	Huntington Hall	Mary Wrench	Head	Unmarried		45	Farmer of 298 Acres, 7 Labours	Cheshire, Stapleford	
		William Wrench	Brother	Unmarried	42			Cheshire, Huntington	
		Ann Wrench	Sister	Unmarried		41		Cheshire, Huntington	
		Eliza Wrench	Sister	Unmarried		40		Cheshire, Huntington	
		James Gunion	Servant	Widower	52		Farm Labourer	Cheshire, Hatton	
		George Price	Servant	Unmarried	24		Farm Labourer	Cheshire, Chorley	
		Thomas Pate	Servant	Unmarried	23		Farm Labourer	Cheshire, Pulford	
		William Ledge	Servant	Unmarried	16		Farm Labourer	Cheshire, Hatton	
		Thomas Roberts	Servant	Unmarried	14		Farm Labourer	Cheshire, Saighton	
		Elisabeth Huxley	Servant	Unmarried		28	House Servant	Cheshire, Churton	
		Margaret Hoyd	Servant	Unmarried		26	House Servant	Cheshire, Churton	
		Mildred Painter	Servant	Unmarried		19	House Servant	Cheshire, Farndon	
16	Porters Heath	Humphrey Lightfoot	Head	Married	42		Farmer of 123 Acres, 1 Labour	Cheshire, Aldersey	
	Farm House	Frances Lightfoot	Wife	Married		38		Cheshire, Barton	
		George Lightfoot	Son	Unmarried	13			Cheshire, Kings Marsh	
		Mary Ann Lightfoot	Daughter	Unmarried		12		Cheshire, Kings Marsh	
		Thomas Lightfoot	Son	Unmarried	10			Cheshire, Kings Marsh	
		Humphrey Lightfoot	Son	Unmarried	8			Cheshire, Kings Marsh	
		Elisabeth Lightfoot	Daughter	Unmarried		6		Cheshire, Huntington	
		John Lightfoot	Son	Unmarried	4			Cheshire, Huntington	
		William Lightfoot	Son	Unmarried	1			Cheshire, Huntington	
		Peter Klyosne	Servant	Unmarried	21		Farm Labourer	Cheshire, Waverton	
17	Cottage	William Huson	Head	Married	28		Agricultural labourer	Cheshire, Huntington	
	Farndon Road	Mary Huson	Wife	Married		27		Cheshire, Bickerton	
		George Huson	Son	Unmar.	0			Cheshire, Huntington	
18	Cottage	James Huson	Head	Married	43		Carter	Cheshire, Huntington	
	Farndon Road	Jane Huson	Wife	Married		44		Cheshire, Mouldsworth	
19	Farmers Arms	William Pheonix	Head	Married	39		Agricultural labourer	Cheshire, Tarvin	
	To Porters Heath	Martha Pheonix	Wife	Married		38		Cheshire, Cowley	
		Richard Pheonix	Son	Unmarried	12			Cheshire, Huntington	
		Ann Pheonix	Daughter	Unmarried		7		Cheshire, Huntington	
		Elizabeth Pheonix	Daughter	Unmarried		2		Cheshire, Huntington	
		Ann Pheonix	Mother	Widow		79		Cheshire, Saighton	

No. of Householder's Schedule	Road, Street Etc. and No. or Name of House	Name and Surname of each Person	Relation to Head of Family	Condition	Age of Male	Age of Female	Rank, Profession or Occupation	Where born	Whether blind, deaf or dumb
34	Butter Beach	John Fleet	Head	Married	35		Farm Bailiff	Waverton, Cheshire	
		Mary Fleet	Wife	Married		35		Spurstow, Cheshire	
		Eliza Lloyd	Servant	Unmarried		17	House Servant	Mold, Flintshire	
35	Huntington Road	William Howell	Head	Married	37		Railway Policeman	Liverpool, Lancashire	
		Emma Howell	Head	Married		43		Huntington, Cheshire	
		Mary H. Howell	Daughter	Unmarried		13		Boughton, Cheshire	
		George Howell	Son		11		Scholar	Boughton, Cheshire	
		Arthur Howell	Son		8		Scholar	Boughton, Cheshire	
		William H. Howell	Son		6		Scholar	Huntington, Cheshire	
		Emma Howell	Daughter			3		Huntington, Cheshire	
		Martha Howell	Daughter			0		Huntington, Cheshire	
36	Rake & Pikel	William Phoenix	Head	Married	47		Beer House Keeper	Tarvin, Cheshire	
		Martha Phoenix	Wife	Married		48		Chowley, Cheshire	
		Richard Phoenix	Son	Unmarried	21		Wheelwright	Huntington, Cheshire	
		Ann Phoenix	Daughter	Unmarried		17		Huntington, Cheshire	
		Elizabeth Phoenix	Daughter	Unmarried		12		Huntington, Cheshire	
		Margaret Phoenix	Daughter			9		Huntington, Cheshire	
		William Phoenix	Son		5			Huntington, Cheshire	
		Ann Phoenix	Mother	Widow		89		Huntington, Cheshire	
37	Rake & Pikel	Daniel Woodcock	Head	Widower	38		Turnpike Gate Keeper	Bretton, Flintshire	
	Toll ---	John Woodcock	Son		15			Broughton, Flintshire	
		Daniel Woodcock	Son		10			Broughton, Flintshire	
		Thomas Woodcock	Son		9			Broughton, Flintshire	
38	Huntington Road	James Hughson	Head	Married	53		Carter at the Railway	Huntington, Cheshire	
		Jane Hughson				57		Tattenhall, Cheshire	
39	Huntington Road	William Hughson	Head	Married	37		Farm Labourer	Huntington, Cheshire	
		Mary Hughson	Wife	Married		36		Huntington, Cheshire	
		George Hughson	Son		11			Huntington, Cheshire	
		John Hughson	Son		5			Huntington, Cheshire	
		Ann Hughson	Daughter			7		Huntington, Cheshire	
		Ann Hughson	Mother			81		Wrexham, Denbighshire	
40	Huntington Hall	Mary Wrench	Head	Unmarried		55	Farmer 296 acres, employs.6 men, 2 boys	Foulk Stapleford, Cheshire	
		Anne Wrench	Sister	Unmarried		51		Huntington, Cheshire	
		Eliza Wrench	Sister	Unmarried		49		Huntington, Cheshire	
		William Wrench	Brother	Unmarried	52			Huntington, Cheshire	
		Elizabeth Burgess	Servant	Unmarried		28	Dairy Maid	Saighton, Cheshire	
		Rebecca Rodgers	Servant	Unmarried		18	House Maid	Sandycroft, Flintshire	
		Martha Vernon	Servant	Unmarried		17	Assistant Dairy Maid	Stapleford, Cheshire	
		Samuel Fleet	Servant	Unmarried	21		Carter	Christleton, Cheshire	
		Samuel Williams	Servant	Unmarried	21		Carter	Boughton, Cheshire	
		William Meacock	Servant	Unmarried	20		Cattle Man	Christleton, Cheshire	
		William Whynne	Servant	Unmarried	15		General Servant	Tarporley, Cheshire	
41	Huntington Road	Joseph B. Colton	Head	Married	34		Farmer of 142 acres, employs 3 men,1 boy	Huntington, Cheshire	
		Jane Colton	Wife	Married		32		Wigan, Lancashire	
		Anne Colton	Daughter			4		Hatton, Cheshire	
		Charles Colton	Son		3			Huntington, Cheshire	
		Ellen Colton	Daughter			1		Huntington, Cheshire	
		Eliza J. Colton	Daughter			0		Huntington, Cheshire	
		George Lockley	Servant	Unmarried	21		Carter	Huntington, Cheshire	
		John Steenes	Servant	Unmarried	25		Cow Man	Boughton, Cheshire	
		William Jones	Servant	Unmarried	15		Stable Boy	Birkenhead, Cheshire	
		Ann Davies	Servant	Widow		65	Nurse	Corwen, Merionethshire	
		Hannah Gauder	Servant	Unmarried		19	Nurse	Chester City	
		Martha Thomas	Servant	Unmarried		17	Housemaid	Huntington, Cheshire	
42	Huntington Road	Ann Thomas	Head	Widow		39	Charwoman	Handley, Cheshire	
		Sarah Thomas	Daughter	Unmarried		14		Huntington, Cheshire	
		Kate Thomas	Daughter			10		Huntington, Cheshire	
		Elizabeth Thomas	Daughter			7		Huntington, Cheshire	
43	Huntington Road	John Smith	Head	Married	51		Labourer	Boughton, Cheshire	
		Ann Smith	Wife	Married		50		Christleton, Cheshire	
		Samuel Smith	Son	Unmarried	21		Bricklayer	Boughton, Cheshire	
		John Smith	Son	Unmarried	20		Labourer	Boughton, Cheshire	
		William Smith	Son		15			Boughton, Cheshire	
		Joseph Smith	Son		11			Boughton, Cheshire	
		Jeremiah Johnson	Father in Law	Widower	73		Labourer	Pavester, Denbighshire	
44	Huntington Road	Frederick Lloyd	Head	Married	35		Game Keeper	Boughton, Cheshire	
		Mary Lloyd	Wife	Married		35		Northop, Flintshire	
		Maria Lloyd	Daughter			9		City of Chester	
		John Lloyd	Son		6			Tarvin Bridge, Cheshire	
		Owen Lloyd	Son		4			Boughton, Cheshire	
		Elizabeth Lloyd	Daughter			2		Huntington, Cheshire	
	Huntington Road	I Uninhabited							
45	Huntington Road	Joseph Barrow	Head	Married	37		Farmer 140 acres, empl.3 men, 1 boy	Prescot, Lancashire	
		Jane Barrow	Wife	Married		43		Prescot, Lancashire	
		Walter J. Barrow	Son		5			Eccleston, Lancashire	
		Samuel Parry	Servant	Unmarried	38		Farm Baliff	Buerton, Cheshire	

No. of Householder's Schedule	Road, Street Etc. and No. or Name of House	Name and Surname of each Person	Relation to Head of Family	Condition	Age of Male	Age of Female	Rank, Profession or Occupation	Where born	Whether blind, deaf or dumb
		James Kelly	Servant	Unmarried	24		Carter	Boughton, Cheshire	
		Martin Griffin	Servant	Unmarried	30		Agricultural labourer	Ballymon, Galway, Ireland	
		James Griffin	Servant	Unmarried	44		Agricultural labourer	Strangforth, Galway, Ireland	
		Elizabeth Morris	Servant	Unmarried		26	Dairymaid	Ludden, Shropshire	
		Mary Preston	Servant	Unmarried		19	Cook	Barnston, Cheshire	
		Mary Davies	Servant	Unmarried		19	Housemaid	Abergele, Denbighshire	
		Ann Denton	Servant	Unmarried		18	Assistant Dairymaid	Boughton, Cheshire	
46	Huntington Road	Sarah Jones	Head	Widow		35	Farmer 240 Acres, empl.2 men	Huntington, Cheshire	
		Thomas Jones	Son		11			Huntington, Cheshire	
		Edward Jones	Son		7			Huntington, Cheshire	
		Elizabeth Jones	Daughter			2		Huntington, Cheshire	
47	Huntington Road	Robert Jones	Head	Married	46		Farm Labourer	Flintshire	
		Sarah Jones	Wife	Married		44		Kinnerton, Flintshire	
48	Chealey Lodge	Thomas Davies	Head	Married	64		Agricultural labourer	Bickerton, Cheshire	
		Sarah Davies	Wife	Married		70		Hargrave, Cheshire	
49	Chealey	John Golborne	Head	Married	58		Farmer of 210 acres	Huntington, Cheshire	
		Emma Golborne	Wife	Married		50		Huntington, Cheshire	
		Ann Golborne	Daughter	Unmarried		23		Huntington, Cheshire	
		Elizabeth Golborne	Daughter	Unmarried		21		Huntington, Cheshire	
		Jane Golborne	Daughter	Unmarried		19		Huntington, Cheshire	
		Sarah Davies	Servant	Unmarried		22	House Servant	Holt, Denbighshire	
		John Andrews	Servant	Unmarried	27		Carter	City of Chester	
		Job Malt	Servant	Unmarried	17		Cow Hand	Hatton, Cheshire	
		William Jones	Servant	Unmarried	15		Groom	Huntington, Cheshire	
50	Eccleston Ferry	James Harnott	Uncle	Widower	76		Ferryman	Huntington, Cheshire	
		Enoch Partington	Head	Married	26		Ferryman	Handley, Cheshire	
		Sarah Partington	Wife	Married		30		Huxley, Cheshire	
		Enoch H. Partington	Son		2			Huntington, Cheshire	
		William T. Partington	Son		0			Huntington, Cheshire	
		Sarah Smith	Servant	Unmarried		13		Longsight, Lancashire	
51		Edward Edwards	Head	Married	49			Denbighshire	
		Jane Edwards	Wife	Married		46		Myfod, Montgomeryshire	
52	Meadow Farm	Samuel Beckett	Head	Unmarried	67		Farmer 196 Acres, empl.2 men	City of Chester	
		Sarah Hughes	Sister	Widow		56		City of Chester	
		Emma Jones	Neice			5		Boughton, Cheshire	
		Sarah Roberts	Servant	Unmarried		46	Dairy Maid	Boughton, Cheshire	
		John Bowkes	Servant	Unmarried	20		Ploughman	Huntington, Cheshire	
		James Pleavin	Servant	Unmarried	14			Boughton, Cheshire	

No. of Householder's Schedule	ROAD, STREET Etc. and No. or NAME of HOUSE	Inhabited	Uninhabited (U.) or Building (B.)	NAME and Surname of each Person	RELATION to Head of Family	CONDITION	Age Male	Age Female	Rank, Profession or OCCUPATION	WHERE BORN	Whether (1) Deaf and Dumb (2) Blind (3) Imbecile or Idiot (4) Lunatic
1	Farm	/		Joseph P. Moore	Head	Married	29		Butcher & Farmer (181acres)	Cheshire, Aldersey	
	Butter Bache			Mary Moore	Wife	Married		29		Lancashire, Liverpool	
	Huntington			George Percy Moore	Son	Unmarried	2			Cheshire, Huntington	
				Joseph Pemberton Moore	Son	Unmarried	0			Cheshire, Huntington	
				George Piercy	Father in Law	Widower	59		Whip Maker (Retired)	Cheshire, Chester	
				Elizabeth Bate	Servant	Unmarried		21	Servant	Cheshire, Macclesfield	
				Ellen Fisher	Servant	Unmarried		14	Servant	Cheshire, Bickerton	
				James Walker	Servant	Unmarried	24		Agricultural labourer	Cheshire, Waverton	
				George O'Niel	Servant	Unmarried	50		Agricultural labourer	Ireland, Castlebar	
2	Farm	/		Thomas Fisher	Head	Married	41		Game Keeper	Cheshire, Bulkeley	
	Butter Bache			Dinah Fisher	Wife	Married		42		Denbighshire, Denbigh	
	Huntington			Joseph Fisher	Son	Unmarried	18		Scholar	Chester, Saltney	
				Thomas Fisher	Son	Unmarried	10		Scholar	Chester, Saltney	
				John Fisher	Son	Unmarried	8		Scholar	Chester, Saltney	
				Alfred Fisher	Son	Unmarried	5		Scholar	Cheshire, Huntington	
				William H. Fisher	Son	Unmarried	1			Cheshire, Huntington	
3	Double House	/		Daniel Woodcock	Head	Married	47		Labourer (18 acres)	Flintshire, Broughton	
	Huntington			Ann Woodcock	Wife	Married		27		Cheshire, Huntington	
				Daniel Woodcock	Son	Unmarried	20		Corn Factor's Afsistant	Flintshire, Broughton	
				Thomas Woodcock	Son	Unmarried	19		Railway Porter	Flintshire, Broughton	
				Alfred Woodcock	Son	Unmarried	2			Cheshire, Huntington	
			/	Edward Edwards	Head	Married	57		Labourer	Montgomeryshire, Welshpool	
				Jane Edwards	Wife	Married		55		Montgomeryshire, Welshpool	
4	Huntington	/		Edward Lockeley	Head	Married	30		Farm Labourer	Cheshire, Huntington	
				Ann Lockeley	Wife	Married		33		Denbighshire, Denbigh	
				Elizabeth Lockeley	Daughter	Unmarried		9	Scholar	Cheshire, Huntington	
				Ann Lockeley	Daughter	Unmarried		3		Cheshire, Huntington	
5	Huntington	/		William Phoenix	Head	Married	56		Labourer, Public.House & 6 acres	Cheshire, Tarvin	
				Martha Phoenix	Wife	Married		52		Cheshire, Chorley Oak	
				Elizabeth Phoenix	Daughter	Unmarried		22	Milliner	Cheshire, Huntington	
				Margaret Phoenix	Daughter	Unmarried		18	At home	Cheshire, Huntington	
				William Geo. Phoenix	Son	Unmarried	14		Scholar	Cheshire, Huntington	
6	Huntington	/		John Salisbury	Head	Married	21		Laborer	Cheshire, Huntington	
				Mary Salisbury	Wife	Married		21		Caernarvonshire, Conway	
				Mary Ellen Salisbury	Daughter			1		Chester	
7	Farm - Huntington	/		Richard Walley	Head	Married	62		Farmer 200 Acres	Cheshire, Utkinton	
				Harriet Walley	Wife	Married		61		Cheshire, Bruen Stapleford	
				Anne Walley	Daughter	Unmarried		31	At home	Cheshire, Saighton	Imbecile from 3 months Old
				Christiana Walley	Gr.daughter	Unmarried		2		London, Middlesex	
				Elizabeth Griffiths	Servant	Unmarried		18	Servant	Denbighshire, Holt	
8	Huntington	/		Joseph Salisbury	Head	Married	31		Labourer	Cheshire, Haverington	
				Mary Salisbury	Wife	Married		31		Cheshire, Christleton	
				Elizabeth Salisbury	Daughter	Unmarried		10	Scholar	Cheshire, Boughton	
				John Salisbury	Son	Unmarried	8		Scholar	Cheshire, Huntington	
				Samuel Salisbury	Son	Unmarried	7		Scholar	Cheshire, Huntington	
				Hannah Salisbury	Daughter	Unmarried		5	Scholar	Cheshire, Huntington	
				Mary Salisbury	Daughter	Unmarried		3	home	Cheshire, Huntington	
				Joseph Salisbury	Son	Unmarried	2		home	Cheshire, Huntington	
				Matthew Salisbury	Son	Unmarried	0		home	Cheshire, Huntington	
9	Farm - Huntington	/		John Goulborn	Head	Married	67		Farmer 169 acres	Cheshire, Huntington	
				Emma Goulborn	Wife	Married		67		Cheshire, Huntington	
				Elizabeth Goulborn	Daughter	Unmarried		31	At home	Cheshire, Huntington	
				Goulborn Tilston	Grandson	Unmarried	11		Scholar	Cheshire, Cotton	
				Joseph Tilston	Grandson	Unmarried	10		Scholar	Cheshire, Cotton	
				Hannah Lloyd	Servant	Unmarried		20	Servant	Cheshire, Pulford	
10	Ferry - Huntington	/		Enoch Partington	Head	Married	36		Ferryman	Cheshire, Goulborn David	
				Sarah Partington	Wife	Married		40		Cheshire, Huxley	
				Harnor Partington	Son	Unmarried	12		Scholar	Cheshire, Huntington	
				William Partington	Son	Unmarried	10		Scholar	Cheshire, Huntington	
				Julia Partington	Daughter	Unmarried		8	Scholar	Cheshire, Huntington	
				Samuel Partington	Son	Unmarried	4		Scholar	Cheshire, Huntington	
				Mary Didsbury	Servant	Unmarried		18	General Servant	Cheshire, Tarvin	
11	Huntington House, Huntington	/		Joseph Barrow	Head	Married	47		Retired Solicitor now farming 150 acres employs 3 labourers	Lancashire, Prescot	
				Jane Barrow	Wife	Married		52		Lancashire, Prescot	
				Walter John Barrow	Son	Unmar.	15		Scholar	Cheshire, Eccleston	
				Ruth Edwards	Servant	Unmar.		23	Housemaid	Flintshire, Mold	
				Hannah Jones	Servant	Unmar.		30	Dairymaid	Flintshire, Holywell	
				William Pugh	Servant	Widower	52		Gardener	Cheshire, Malpas	
				John Salisbury	Servant	Unmar.	22		Coachman	Lancashire, Manchester	
12	Cottage - Huntington	/		Samuel Parry	Head	Married	50		Farm Bailiff	Cheshire, Huntington	
				Ellen Ann Parry	Wife	Married		29		Chester	
				Ann Parry	Daughter	Unmarried		1		Cheshire, Huntington	
				William Anderson	Lodger	Widower	60		Cow Man	Ireland	
13	Farm - Huntington	/		Mary Wrench	Head	Unmarried		65	Farmer 297 Acres	Cheshire, Stapleford	
				Eliza Wrench	Sister	Unmarried		60		Cheshire, Huntington	
				William Wrench	Brother	Unmarried	62		On Farm	Cheshire, Huntington	
				Samuel Parry	Servant	Unmarried	23		Farm Servant	Cheshire, Saighton	
				John Hughson	Servant	Unmarried	16		Farm Servant	Cheshire, Huntington	
				Joseph Dason	Servant	Unmarried	14		Farm Servant	Cheshire, Saighton	
				Harriet Pover	Servant	Unmarried		24	Dairy Maid	Flintshire, Wrexham	
				Fanny Lloyd	Servant	Unmarried		14	General Servant	Cheshire, Poulton	
14	Farm - Huntington		/	Samuel Cartwright	Head	Unmarried	40		Farm (120 acres) employs 2 Labourers	Chester	
				Elizabeth Roberts	Servant	Unmarried		46	General Servant	N. Wales, Bala	
				Samuel Salisbury	Servant	Unmarried	54		Farm Servant	Cheshire, Waverton	
15	Cottage - Huntington		/	William Hughson	Head	Married	45		Laborer	Cheshire, Huntington	
				Mary Hughson	Wife	Married		44		Cheshire, Bickerton	

| No. of Householder's Schedule | ROAD, STREET Etc. and No. or NAME of HOUSE | HOUSES | | NAME and Surname of each Person | RELATION to Head of Family | CONDITION | AGE of | | Rank, Profession or OCCUPATION | WHERE BORN | Whether (1) Deaf and Dumb (2) Blind (3) Imbecile or Idiot (4) Lunatic |
		Inhabited	Uninhabited (U.) or Building (B.)				Male	Female			
				Ann Hughson	Daughter	Unmarried		18	At home	Cheshire, Huntington	
				Elizabeth Hughson	Daughter	Unmarried		7	At home	Cheshire, Huntington	
16	Cottage - Huntington			James Hughson	Head	Married	66		Laborer	Cheshire, Huntington	
				Jane Hughson	Wife	Married		68		Cheshire, Mouldsworth	
17	Toll House - Huntington	/		Joseph Roberts	Head	Married	48		Laborer & Toll Keeper	Cheshire, Pulford	
				Elizabeth Roberts	Wife	Married		42	Attend Toll gate	Denbighshire, Gresford	
				Mercy Louisa Roberts	Daughter			10	Scholar	Denbighshire, Rofsett	
				Alfred Roberts	Son		4		At home	Cheshire, Lache	
18	Cottage - Huntington	/		William Howell	Head	Married	45		Labourer	Lancashire, Liverpool	
				Emma Howell	Wife	Married		45		Cheshire, Huntington	
				Arthur Howell	Son	Unmarried	19		Labourer	Cheshire, Great Boughton	
				William Howell	Son	Unmarried	16		Errand Boy	Cheshire, Huntington	
				Emma Howell	Daughter	Unmarried		13	Scholar	Cheshire, Huntington	
				Martha Howell	Daughter	Unmarried		9	Scholar	Cheshire, Huntington	
				Ann Howell	Daughter	Unmarried		8	Scholar	Cheshire, Huntington	
				Eliza Howell	Daughter	Unmarried		4	At home	Cheshire, Huntington	
19	Cottage - Huntington	/		Robert Jones	Head	Married	56		Carter	Flintshire, Hope	
				Sarah Jones	Wife	Married		54	House duties	Flintshire, Kinnerton	
				William Jones	Son	Unmarried	25		Bricklayer	Cheshire, Chealey	
				James Roberts	Lodger	Unmarried	29		Carter	Cheshire, Nantwich	
20	Farm - Huntington	/		William Wharton	Head	Married	40		Farmer 137 acres employs 4 labourers	Cheshire, Burwardsley	
				Ellen Wharton	Wife	Married		38		Cheshire, Bulkeley	
				Ann Wharton	Daughter	Unmarried		19	At home	Cheshire, Bulkeley	
				Sarah Jane Wharton	Daughter	Unmarried		11	Scholar	Cheshire, Burwardsley	
				William Wharton	Son	Unmarried	2			Cheshire, Huntington	
				Maria Fisher	Mother in Law	Widow		70		Chester	
				Emma White	Servant	Unmarried		18	General Domestic Servant	Cheshire, Birkenhead	
				Mary Manning	Servant	Unmarried		14	General Domestic Servant	Cheshire, Bulkeley	
				William Salisbury	Servant	Unmarried	19		Farm Servant	Cheshire, Huntington	
				Alfred Wharton	Servant	Unmarried	14		Farm Servant	Cheshire, Saighton	
				George Gregory	Labourer	Widower	55		Farm Labourer	Cheshire, Saighton	
21	Cottage - Huntington	/		William Lloyd	Head	Married	56		Labourer	Cheshire, Saighton	
				Ann Lloyd	Wife	Married		45		Cheshire, Hanley	

No. of Householder's Schedule	ROAD, STREET Etc. and No. or NAME of HOUSE	Inhabited	Uninhabited (U.) or Building (B.)	NAME and Surname of each Person	RELATION to Head of Family	CONDITION as to Marriage	Age of Male	Age of Female	Rank, Profession or OCCUPATION	WHERE BORN	If (1) Deaf and Dumb (2) Blind (3) Imbecile or Idiot (4) Lunatic
68	Cheadle Lodge	/		Robert Jones	Head	Married	66		Agricultural Labourer	Hope, Flintshire	
				Sarah Jones	Wife	Married		63		Hope, Flintshire	
				William Jones	Son	Married	34		Bricklayer	Saighton, Cheshire	
				Hannah Jones	Daughter-in-Law	Married		29		Saighton, Cheshire	
				Robert Jones	Grandson		6		Scholar	Saighton, Cheshire	
				Agnes E. Jones	Granddaughter			4	Scholar	Saighton, Cheshire	
				Ada Jones	Granddaughter			2	Scholar	Saighton, Cheshire	
69	Cheadle	/		Thomas Salmon	Head	Married	41		Farmer of 482 acres employs 1 labourer 2 boys	Huntington, Cheshire	
				Eliza Salmon	Wife	Married		27		Farndon, Cheshire	
				Eliza Salmon	Daughter			5	Scholar	Huntington, Cheshire	
				Sarah Salmon	Daughter			1		Huntington, Cheshire	
				Joseph Dutton	Servant	Unmarried	19		General Servant Outdoors	Stableford, Cheshire	
				John Jones	Servant	Unmarried	19		General Servant Indoors	Aldford, Cheshire	
				Elizabeth A. Locket	Servant	Unmarried		17	General Servant Domestic	Ashton, Cheshire	
				Sarah Edge	Servant	Unmarried		13	General Servant Domestic	Waverton, Cheshire	
70	Eaton Ferry	/		Enoch Partington	Head	Married	46		Farmer of 70 Acres	Handley, Cheshire	
				Sarah Partington	Wife	Married		50	Farmer's wife	Huxley, Cheshire	
				William Partington	Son	Unmarried	20		Farmer's son	Eaton Ferry, Cheshire	
				Julia Partington	Daughter	Unmarried		18	Farmer's daughter	Eaton Ferry, Cheshire	
				Samuel Partington	Son	Unmarried	14		Farmer's son	Eaton Ferry, Cheshire	
				Annie Molyneux	Servant	Unmarried		17	General Servant Domestic	Saughall, Cheshire	
71		/		Richard D. Walley	Head	Married	38		Farmer employs 2 men	Saighton, Cheshire	
				Annie S. Walley	Wife	Married		38	Farmer's wife	Eaton by Tarporley, Cheshire	
				Alice Harriet Walley	Daughter	Unmarried		9	Scholar	Christleton, Cheshire	
				Lillian M. Walley	Daughter	Unmarried		7	Scholar	Huntington, Cheshire	
				Jane E. Walley	Daughter	Unmarried		6	Scholar	Huntington, Cheshire	
				Charles J. Walley	Son		4			Huntington, Cheshire	
				Richard W. Walley	Son		1			Huntington, Cheshire	
				Ester Kennedy	Servant	Unmarried		19	Domestic Servant	Chester, Cheshire	
72	Huntington House	/		John Large	Head	Married	30		Farm Bailiff of 139 Acres	Bunbury, Cheshire	
				Williamina W. Large	Wife	Married		27	Farm Bailiff's wife	Birkenhead, Cheshire	
				Joseph Bateman	Servant	Unmarried	16		Farm Servant Indoors	Marbury, Cheshire	
				Hugh Ashley	Servant	Unmarried	18		Farm Servant Indoors	Grindley Brook,Whitchurch,Shropshire	
73	Huntington Road	/		John Dutton	Head	Married	23		Farm Labourer	Huntington, Cheshire	
				Kate Dutton	Wife	Married		25	Farm Labourer's wife	Waverton, Cheshire	
74		/		Thomas Dutton	Head	Married	60		Agricultural Labourer	Handley, Cheshire	
				Elizabeth Dutton	Wife	Married		65	Agricultural Labourer's wife	Coddington, Cheshire	
				George Dutton	Son	Unmarried	22		Joiner	Handley, Cheshire	
75		/		Edward Lockley	Head	Married	38		Agricultural Labourer	Huntington, Cheshire	
				Ann Lockley	Wife	Married		39	Agricultural Labourer's wife	Denbigh, North Wales	
				Ann Lockley	Daughter	Unmarried		12	Scholar	Huntington, Cheshire	
				Fanny Lockley	Daughter	Unmarried		4		Huntington, Cheshire	
				Annie E. Bentley	Nurse Child			5		Boughton, Cheshire	
76	Aldford Road	/		William Lloyd	Head	Married	66		General Labourer Out of Employ	Saighton, Cheshire	
				Ann Lloyd	Wife	Married		56	Labourer's wife	Handley, Cheshire	
				Mary A. Thomas	Visitor			4	Scholar	Aldford, Cheshire	
				Henry Ward	Lodger	Married	30		Farm Labourer	Yorkshire	
				Ellen Ward	Lodger	Married		24	Formerly Dairymaid	Malpas, Cheshire	
77		/		Henry Farnsworth	Head	Married	28		Manager of Farm 118 Acres	Dunkinfield, Lancashire	
				Sarah Farnsworth	Wife	Married		23	Manager's wife	Chester, Cheshire	
				Sarah Farnsworth	Daughter	Unmarried		6	Manager's daughter	Chester, Cheshire	
				Charles Farnsworth	Son	Unmarried	4		Manager's son	Chester, Cheshire	
				Gertrude Farnsworth	Daughter	Unmarried		1	Manager's daughter	Chester, Cheshire	
				Ellen Jones	Servant	Unmarried		51	Domestic General Servant	Saighton, Cheshire	
				Henry Swindly	Servant	Unmarried	18		Farm Servant Indoors	Stableford, Cheshire	
				George Rigby	Lodger	Married	47		Engineer RW Retired	Chester, Cheshire	
				Diana Rigby	Lodger	Married		41	Lodger's wife	Deavonport, Devonshire	
78	Huntington Hall	/		John Akitt	Head	Married	35		Farmer of 295 Acres employs 4 Labourers	Bassenthwaite, Cumberland	
				Hannah Akitt	Wife	Married		31	Farmer's wife	Brigham, Cumberland	
				John Akitt	Son	Unmarried	7		Scholar	Mosser, Cumberland	
				Mary Akitt	Daughter	Unmarried		6	Scholar	Mosser, Cumberland	
				Wilson Akitt	Son	Unmarried	3			Mosser, Cumberland	
				Annie M. Akitt	Daughter			0		Mosser, Cumberland	
				Margaret Ramsey	Servant	Unmarried		23	General Servant	Scotland	
				John Barwise	Servant		19		Farm Servant Indoors	Clifton, Cumberland	
				Mossop Chester	Servant	Unmarried	18		Farm Servant Indoors	Egremont, Cumberland	
				Patrick Cunningham	Servant	Married	44		Farm Servant Indoors	Ireland	
79	Ivy Cottage	/		William Hurson	Head	Married	56		Agricultural Labourer	Huntington, Cheshire	
				Mary Hurson	Wife	Married		55	Agricultural Labourer's wife	Broxton, Cheshire	
				Arthur Stonley	Border	Unmarried	6		Scholar	Broxton, Cheshire	
80		/		Samuel Roberts	Head	Married	43		Game Keeper	Oscroft, Cheshire	
				John Roberts	Son	Married	23		Bricklayer	Stallins, Flint, Wales	
81	Rake & Pikel	/		William Phoenix	Head	Married	60		Agricultural Labourer	Tarvin, Cheshire	
				Martha Phoenix	Wife	Married		59	Agricultural Labourer's wife	Chorley, Cheshire	
				Alfred Woodcock	Grandson			12	Scholar	Huntington, Cheshire	
82	Meadow Farm	/		Richard Duckers	Head	Married	59		Farmer of 61 Acres	Malpas, Cheshire	
				Margaret Duckers	Wife	Married		53	Farmer's wife	Worthenbury, Flintshire	
				Emily Duckers	Daughter	Unmarried		18	Farmer's daughter	Malpas, Cheshire	
				William Dutton	Servant	Unmarried	20		General Labourer	Chester, Cheshire	
				Sid Laker	Servant	Unmarried	16		General Labourer	Chester, Cheshire	
83	Aldford Road	/		William Howell	Head	Widower	57		Agricultural Labourer	Liverpool, Lancashire	
				William Howell	Son	Unmarried	26		General Labourer	Huntington, Cheshire	
				William Phoenix	Son in Law	Married	25		Wheelwright	Huntington, Cheshire	
				Emma Phoenix	Daughter	Married		23	Wheelwright's wife	Huntington, Cheshire	
				George Phoenix	Grandson		0			Huntington, Cheshire	
84	Aldford Road	/		Daniel Woodcock	Head	Married	55		Agricultural Labourer	Broughton, Flintshire	
				Ann Woodcock	Wife	Married		37		Huntington, Cheshire	
				Elizabeth Woodcock	Daughter	Unmarried		2		Bradley, Shropshire	
				Fredrick Woodcock	Son	Unmarried	1			Huntington, Cheshire	
				Mary Woodcock	Daughter	Married		25		Broughton, Flintshire	
				John Woodcock	Grandson	Unmarried	4			Aldford, Cheshire	
				David Woodcock	Son	Married	30			Huntington, Cheshire	
85	Butter Beach	/		John Moore	Head	Married	50		Butcher & Farmer	Aldersey, Cheshire	
				Letitia Moore	Wife	Married		27	Butcher's wife	Stanney, Cheshire	

No. of Householder's Schedule	ROAD, STREET Etc. and No. or NAME of HOUSE	HOUSES Inhabited	Uninhabited (U.) or Building (B.)	NAME and Surname of each Person	RELATION to Head of Family	CONDITION as to Marriage	Age of Male	Age of Female	Rank, Profession or OCCUPATION	WHERE BORN	If (1) Deaf and Dumb (2) Blind (3) Imbecile or Idiot (4) Lunatic
				Emma Moore	Daughter	Unmarried		19	Butcher's daughter	Chester, Cheshire	
				Ellen Moore	Daughter	Unmarried		8	Scholar	Chester, Cheshire	
				William Moore	Son	Unmarried	5		Scholar	Chester, Cheshire	
				Lousia Moore	Daughter	Unmarried		4		Chester, Cheshire	
				Edith M. Moore	Daughter	Unmarried		2		Bradley, Cheshire	
				Eliza Moore	Daughter	Unmarried		0		Huntington, Cheshire	
				John Simpson	Servant	Unmarried	41		Farm Servant Indoors	Bradley, Cheshire	
				Joseph Pleavin	Servant	Unmarried	23		Farm Servant Indoors	Christleton, Cheshire	
				Job Cotgreve	Servant	Unmarried	18		Farm Servant Indoors	Barrow, Cheshire	
				Catherine Kelly	Servant	Unmarried		18	General Servant	Tipperary, Ireland	
86	Porters Heath	/		Joseph Windsor	Head	Married	27		Farm Labourer	Bickerton, Cheshire	
				Mary Windsor	Wife	Married		27		Bickerton, Cheshire	
				Robert Windsor	Son		6		Scholar	Bickerton, Cheshire	
				Joseph Windsor	Son		3			Bickerton, Cheshire	
87		/		Samuel Parry	Head	Widower	60		Farm Labourer	Aldford, Cheshire	
88		/		Joseph Salisbury	Head	Married	41		General Labourer	Aldford, Cheshire	
				Mary Salisbury	Wife	Married		41	General Labourer's wife	Christleton, Cheshire	
				Samuel Salisbury	Son	Unmarried	17		General Labourer	Huntington, Cheshire	
				Mary Salisbury	Daughter			13	Scholar	Huntington, Cheshire	
				Joseph Salisbury	Son		12		Scholar	Huntington, Cheshire	
				Martha Salisbury	Daughter			11	Scholar	Huntington, Cheshire	
				Alice Salisbury	Daughter			9	Scholar	Huntington, Cheshire	
				William Salisbury	Son		5			Huntington, Cheshire	
				George Melton	Lodger	Married	21		General Labourer	Norfolk	
				Elizabeth Melton	Wife	Married		20	General Labourer's wife	Boughton, Cheshire	
				Edith Melton	Daughter			0		Huntington, Cheshire	

1	2	HOUSES		5	6	7	8	9	10	11	12	13	14	15	16
No. of Householder's Schedule	Name of Street, Place or Road and Name or No. of House	Inhabited	Uninhabited (U.) or Building (B.)	Number of Rooms Occupied, if less than five	Name and Surname of each Person who abode in the house, on the Night of 30th March, 1851	Relation to Head of Family	Condition	Male	Female	Rank, Profession or Occupation	Employer	Employed	Neither Employer or Employed	Where born	(1) Deaf and Dumb (2) Blind (3) Lunatic, Imbecile or Idiot
44		/		2	James Latimer	Head	Single	48		Labourer General		x		Yorkshire	
45		/			William Phoenix	Head	Married	79		Agricultural Labourer		x		Cheshire, Tarvin	
					Martha Phoenix	Wife	Married		75					Cheshire, Chowley	
				4	Ann Woodcock	Daughter	Widow		45	General Servant Domestic				Cheshire, Huntington	
					Elizabeth Woodcock	Granddaughter	Single		12	Scholar				Cheshire, Huntington	
46		/			William Howell	Head	Widower	67		Labourer (General)		x		Lancashire, Liverpool	
					William Phoenix	Son-in-Law	Married	35		Wheelwright	x			Cheshire, Huntington	
					Emma Phoenix	Daughter	Married		32					Cheshire, Huntington	
					George Phoenix	Grandson	Single	10		Scholar				Cheshire, Huntington	
					Alfred Phoenix	Grandson	Single	8		Scholar				Cheshire, Huntington	
					William Phoenix	Grandson	Single	7		Scholar				Cheshire, Saighton	
47		/			Joseph Dutton	Head	Married	27		Labourer		x		Cheshire, Aldford	
					Mary Dutton	Wife	Married		23					Cheshire, Aldford	
					Annie Dutton	Daughter	Single		1					Cheshire, Bruera	
					Jane Dutton	Neice	Single		10	Scholar				Cheshire, Chester	
48		/			John Jones	Head	Married	51		Farmer	x			Lancashire, Liverpool	
					Harriett Jones	Wife	Married		46					Cheshire, Chester	
					Josephine Jones	Daughter	Single		17	Farmer's daughter				Cheshire, Chester	
					Evangeline Jones	Daughter	Single		18	Farmer's daughter				Cheshire, Chester	
					John Herbert Jones	Son	Single	15		Farmer's son				Cheshire, Chester	
					Joseph Smathers	Servant	Single	36		Labourer		x		Ireland	
					Martin Bradey	Servant	Single	25		Gardener		x		Flintshire, Shotton	
49		/			John Roberts	Head	Married	33		Gamekeeper		x		Cheshire, Hargrave	
					Charlotte Roberts	Wife	Married		32					Manchester, Salford	
					Charlotte Ethel Roberts	Daughter	Single		11	Scholar				Cheshire, Oscroft	
					Horace Roberts	Son	Single	9		Scholar				Cheshire, Huntington	
					Mary Catherine Roberts	Daughter	Single		2					Cheshire, Huntington	
50		/			William Hewson	Head	Married	68		Wheelwright		x		Cheshire, Huntington	
				3	Mary Hewson	Wife	Married		59					Cheshire, Huntington	
					Hugh Ashley	Son-in-Law	Married	28		Agricultural Labourer		x		Cheshire, Huntington	
					Elizabeth Ashley	Daughter	Married		27					Cheshire, Huntington	
					Arthur Ashley	Grandson		2						Cheshire, Huntington	
					Sarah Ann Ashley	Granddaughter			0					Cheshire, Huntington	
51	Huntington Hall	/			John Akitt	Head	Married	44		Farmer	x			Cumberland, Bassinthwaite	
					Hannah Akitt	Wife	Married		41					Cumberland, Brigham	
					John Akitt	Son	Single	17						Cumberland, Brigham	
					Mary Akitt	Daughter	Single		16					Cumberland, Brigham	
					Wilson Akitt	Son	Single	13		Scholar				Cumberland, Brigham	
					Alice Akitt	Daughter			8	Scholar				Cheshire, Bruera	
					Bill Towers	Servant	Single	30		Agricultural Labourer		x		Cheshire, Chester	
					George Parker	Servant	Single	22		Agricultural Labourer		x		Cheshire, Chester	
					Lawrence Cunningham	Servant	Single	24		Agricultural Labourer		x		Ireland	
					David Latimer	Servant	Single	44		Agricultural Labourer		x		Ireland	
					Mary Eliza Scott	Servant	Single		22	Servant (Domestic) General		x		Huntingtonshire, Abbots Ripton	
					Alice Salisbury	Servant	Single		18	Servant (Domestic) Housemaid		x		Cheshire, Bruera	
52		/			John Moore	Head	Married	60		Farmer	X			Cheshire, Aldersey	
					Letitia Moore	Wife	Married		35					Cheshire, Stanney	
					Ellen Moore	Daughter	Single		18					Cheshire, Chester	
					William Henry Moore	Son	Single	15						Cheshire, Chester	
					Louise Moore	Daughter	Single		14					Cheshire, Chester	
					Edith Moore	Daughter			12	Scholar				Cheshire, Bradley	
					Margaret Moore	Daughter			9	Scholar				Cheshire, Huntington	
					Albert Moore	Son		7		Scholar				Cheshire, Huntington	
					Letitia Moore	Daughter			3					Cheshire, Huntington	
					George Moore	Son		2						Cheshire, Huntington	
					Amy Moore	Daughter			0					Cheshire, Huntington	
					John Simpson	Servant	Single	45		Agricultural Labourer		x		Cheshire, Bradley	
					John Hughes	Servant	Single	24		Agricultural Labourer		x		Flintshire, Mold	
53		/			Ellen Powell	Servant			64	Housekeeper		x		Cheshire, Dodleston	
				4	John Tinn	Servant		18		Farm Servant		x		Ireland, Roscommon	
					John Hopkins	Servant		18		Farm Servant		x		Ireland, Mayer	
54		/			Hannah Speed	Wife	Married		25					Cheshire, Saighton	
					Thomas Speed	Son		1						Cheshire, Saighton	
				3	Joseph Speed	Son		1						Cheshire, Saighton	
					Isaac Speed	Son		0						Cheshire, Saighton	
55		/			John Bithell	Head	Married	41		Woodman		x			
					Fanny Bithell	Wife	Married		48					Cheshire, Thornton le Moors	
				2	Joseph Bithell	Son		13		Scholar				Cheshire, Hargrave	
					William Bithell	Son		12		Scholar				Lancashire, Bolton	
56		/			Samuel Gilliam	Head	Married	59		Labourer (Builders)		x		Cheshire, Chester (Den.Molli)	
					Mary Gilliam	Wife	Married		55					Flintshire, Sealand	
					Joseph Gilliam	Son	Single	25		Labourer (Builders)		x		Denbighshire, Lavister	
					Edward Gilliam	Son	Single	22		Agricultural Labourer		x		Denbighshire, Lavister	
					Job Gilliam	Son	Single	19		Labourer (Builders)		x		Denbighshire, Lavister	
					Arthur Gilliam	Son		13		Scholar				Cheshire, Churton	
					Noah Gilliam	Son		8		Scholar				Cheshire, Huntington	
				2	Tom Gilliam	Son		8		Scholar				Cheshire, Huntington	
					Herbert Gilliam	Son		4		Scholar				Cheshire, Huntington	
57		/			Thomas Henry Parker	Head	Single	34		Farmer	x			Cheshire, Aldford	
					Mary Thomas	Servant	Single		68	Housekeeper (Domestic)		x		Denbighshire, Holt	
					Thomas Callaghan	Servant	Single	19		Farm Servant		x		Ireland, Roscommon	
58		/			Richard Dutton Walley	Head	Married	48		Farmer	x			Cheshire, Saighton	
					Annie Lydia Walley	Wife	Married		48					Cheshire, Eton	
					Annie Walley	Sister	Single		50					Cheshire, Saighton	
					Alice Harriett Walley	Daughter	Single		20	Farmer's daughter				Cheshire, Christleton	
					Lilian Mary Walley	Daughter	Single		18	Farmer's daughter				Cheshire, Huntington	
					Jane Ethel Walley	Daughter	Single		16	Farmer's daughter				Cheshire, Huntington	
					Charles John Walley	Son		15		Farmer's son				Cheshire, Huntington	
					Richard Wallace Walley	Son		12		Scholar				Cheshire, Huntington	
					Francis Dutton Walley	Son		9		Scholar				Cheshire, Huntington	
					Annie Ethel Wormall	Niece			15					Flintshire, Oswestry	
					Thomas Pleavin	Servant	Widower	73		Assistant Labourer		x		Cheshire, Saighton	
					Samuel Hignett	Servant	Single	16		Farm Servant		x		Cheshire, Saighton	

No. of Householder's Schedule	Name of Street, Place or Road and Name or No. of House	HOUSES			Number of Rooms Occupied, if less than five	Name and Surname of each Person who abode in the house, on the Night of 30th March, 1851	Relation to Head of Family	Condition	Age of		Rank, Profession or Occupation	Employer	Employed	Neither Employer or Employed	Where born	(1) Deaf and Dumb (2) Blind (3) Lunatic, Imbecile or idiot
		Inhabited	Uninhabited (U.) or Building (B.)						Male	Female						
						Charles Bebbington	Servant	Single	14		Farm Servant		x		Cheshire, Handley	
59	Cheaveley Farm	/				Thomas Salmon	Head	Married	51		Farmer	x			Cheshire, Huntington	
						Eliza Salmon	Wife	Married		37					Cheshire, Farndon	
						Mary Eliza Salmon	Daughter	Single		15					Cheshire, Huntington	
						Sarah Salmon	Daughter	Single		11	Scholar				Cheshire, Huntington	
						Robert Salmon	Son		8		Scholar				Cheshire, Huntington	
						Alfred Phillips	Servant	Single	21		Farm Servant		x		Cheshire, Chowley	
						William Smith	Servant	Single	18		Farm Servant		x		Suffolk, Little Turlow	
						Alice Painter	Servant	Single		21	Servant (Domestic) General		x		Cheshire, Farndon	
						Mary Powell	Servant	Single		19	Servant (Domestic) General		x		Cheshire, Chester	
60	Boat Farm	/				Enoch Partington	Head	Married	56		Farmer	x			Cheshire, Handley	
						Sarah Partington	Wife	Married		32					Cheshire, Chester	
						Samuel Partington	Son	Single	24		Farmer	x			Cheshire, Huntington	
						Eddy Dutton	Servant	Single	20		Farm Servant		x		Lancashire, Poulton le Fylde	
						Sarah Steen	Servant	Single		25	Servant (Domestic)		x		Cheshire, Aldford	
						Elizabeth Formston	Servant	Single		16	Servant (Domestic)		x		Cheshire, Handley	
						Elizabeth Bithell	Servant	Single		16	Servant (Domestic)		x		Cheshire, Handley	

BIBLIOGRAPHY

MANUSCRIPT COLLECTIONS

| The Hincks Collection | Cheshire Record Office | ZD / HINCKS. The private records of a local landholding family containing various correspondence and plans in connection with the running of their estate. |
| The Grosvenor Archives | Chester City Record Office | MAPS & PLANS, BOX R. The Eaton Estate records belonging to the Duke of Westminster which include maps, plans, scheduled deeds and indentures |
| Local Authority Archives | Cheshire Record Office | TRT – Turnpike Trust records RGT – Huntington Valuation Lists, QDV – Land Tax for Lea Newbold,

EDT – Saighton Tithe Map, EDP, MF, EDA, P24, DDX - Bruera church records, SL 122 – Saighton a School Log Book,

SL 60 – Huntington School Log Book |

PAMPHLETS AND PERIODICALS

| *The Cheshire Sheaf* | Cheshire Record Office and Chester Library |

HISTORIES AND ACCOUNTS

Bagshaw, Samuel   *History, Gazetteer & Directory of Cheshire, 1850*

Beck, J.   *Tudor Cheshire*   Cheshire Community Council, Chester1968

Bovill, E. W.   *English Country Life 1780-1830*   Oxford University Press, 1962

Bretherton, F. F.   *Early Methodism in and around Chester 1749-1812*   Phillipson & Golder, Chester, 1903

Burne, R. V. H.   *Chester Cathedral*   S. P. C. K., London, 1958
Burne, R. V. H.   *The Monks of Chester*   S. P. C. K., London 1962
Cheshire County Council   *Population Changes in Cheshire, 1946-69*

Cheshire County Council   *Our Cheshire Parishes*   Cheshire, 1994

Crosby, A.   *A History of Cheshire*   Phillimore Co. Ltd., Chichester, 1996
Davies, C. S.   *The Agricultural History of Cheshire 1750-1850*   Chetham Society, Manchester, 1960

Dodgson, J. McN.   *The Place-names of Cheshire, Parts III, IV*   Cambridge University Press, 1971, 1972, 1977
Dore, R. N.   *The Civil Wars in Cheshire*   Cheshire Community Council, Chester, 1966
Gastrell, Bishop   *Notitia Cestriensis*   Chetham Society, Vol. 8, 1st. Series

Harris, B. E., Ed.   *The Victoria History of the County of Chester, Vols. I, II & III*   Oxford University Press, Oxford, 1979, 1980 & 1987

Hodson, J. H.   *Cheshire, 1660-1780: Restoration to Industrial Revolution*   Cheshire Community Council, Chester, 1978
Johnson, J. H.   *Suburban Growth*   Wiley, London, 1974

Jones, E. L. & Mingay, J. D.   *Land, Labour & Population in the Industrial Revolution*   E. Arnold Ltd., London, 1967
Lysons, D. & S.   *Magna Britannia, vol. II. Part II. : The County Palatine of Chester.*   London, 1810

Mercer, W. B.	*A Survey of the Agriculture of Cheshire*	Royal Agric. Soc., London, 1963
Morris, J. Gen.Ed.	*Domesday Book, Cheshire*	Phillimore, Chichester, 1978
Morris, R. H	*Chester*	S. P. C. K., London, 1895
Morris, R. H.	*The Siege of Chester 1643-1646*	Chester, 1924
Oliver, P	*Dunroamin: the suburban semi and its enemies*	Pimlico, 1994
Ormerod, G.	*The History of the County Palatine and City of Chester, 3 vols. Helsby Ed.*	
Pevsner, N. & Hubbard, E.	*The Buildings of England CHESHIRE*	Penguin Books, Middlesex, 1978
Phillips, C. B. & Smith, J. H.	*Lancashire and Cheshire from AD 1540*	Longman, 1994
Richards, R.	*Old Cheshire Churches*	E.J. Morten, Manchester, 1973
Richardson, R. C.	*Puritanism in North-West England*	University Press, Manchester, 1972
Scard, G	*Squire and Tenant: Rural Life in Cheshire 1760 – 1900*	Cheshire Community Council, Chester, 1980
Sylvester, D. & Nulty, G.	*The Historical Atlas of Cheshire*	Cheshire Community Council, Chester, 1958